EVERYTHING IS TERRIBLE.

MATTHEW DiBENEDETTI

Author of *I Hate Everything.*

Adams Media

New York • London • Toronto • Sydney • New Delhi

adamsmedia

Adams Media
An Imprint of Simon & Schuster, Inc.
57 Littlefield Street
Avon, Massachusetts 02322

First Adams Media trade paperback edition September 2020

Interior design by Sylvia McArdle
Illustrations by Elisabeth Lariviere; © 123RF

Manufactured in the United States of America

10 9 8 7 6 5 4 3 2 1

Library of Congress Cataloging-in-Publication Data
Names: DiBenedetti, Matthew, author.
Title: Everything is terrible. / Matthew DiBenedetti, author of I hate everything.
Description: First Adams Media trade paperback edition. | Avon, Massachusetts: Adams Media, 2020.
Identifiers: LCCN 2020017450 | ISBN 9781507213629 (pb) | ISBN 9781507213650 (ebook)
Subjects: LCSH: Conduct of life--Humor. | Pessimism--Humor.
Classification: LCC PN6231.C6142 D5275 2020 | DDC 818/.602--dc23
LC record available at https://lccn.loc.gov/2020017450

ISBN 978-1-5072-1362-9
ISBN 978-1-5072-1365-0 (ebook)

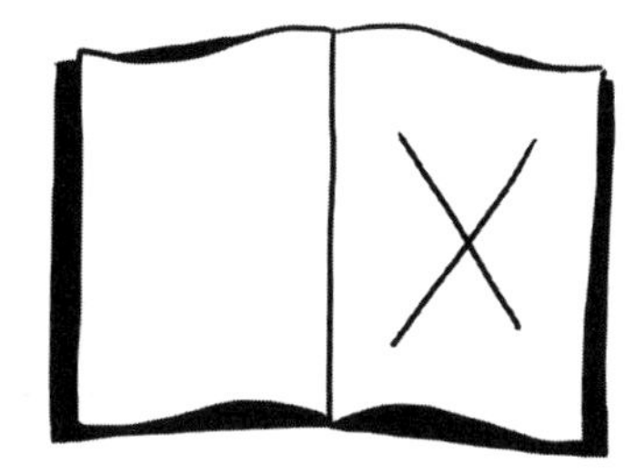

Dedication

Everything is terrible, so NOBODY should expect this book to be dedicated to them.

Introduction

It wasn't always like this. The world used to be a shiny, happy place, filled with promise. But not anymore. Let's be honest: You've seen it happen before your very own eyes. Everything—and I mean absolutely ***everything***—has gotten worse, and is now terrible. You know it's true. Just think about it....

It's terrible that people now pay for graffiti art.

It's terrible that people don't reshare their ***Netflix*** password after they changed it.

It's terrible that they don't sell Girl Scout Cookies all year long.

It's terrible how many people simply lack common sense.

It's terrible how easily frustrated you've become with all of the idiotic behavior.

It's terrible that our world is going down the wrong path.

It's terrible that you can't find the right path without a GPS app.

It's terrible that you had to delete that app because your phone ran out of space...again.

It's terrible that AI like Siri and Alexa rely on the Internet for true information.

It's terrible that everything is terrible.

And it's terrible that misery loves company. But it does, so in this book you'll not only find a place to commiserate about life's everyday frustrations; you'll also find prompts for nearly one hundred terribly fun activities crafted just for our kind of dark amusement. You won't find any rules here, so feel free to use this book however you see fit. Do the activities in any order. Flip to the pages that you find most interesting. And realize that we're all in this terrible situation together.

Or don't.

It's terrible when other people try to tell you what to do.

It’s terrible when things are so terrible you just have to laugh.

It’s terrible that we watch movies that make us cry.

It’s terrible when a good commercial makes you cry.

It’s terrible that we have go-to songs to listen to when we are down.

HA HA HA HA HA HA HA HA HA HA

It’s terrible when you hear a great song so many times…
you begin to hate it.

Worst Songs Ever.

It's terrible that every rose has its thorn.
It's terrible that the 80s will never return.
It's terrible that, like my parents, I now say, "Music was so much better when I was younger."
It's terrible that I own tons of music, but none of it is tangible.
It's terrible that tangible music takes up so much space.
It's terrible when someone flips through my phone's music catalog and comes across the one song that I'm embarrassed to love.

For as many great songs as there are that get us going, there are so many terrible songs that, for some reason, we can't turn off fast enough. Make a playlist on the following iTunes app screen for every song and music artist that you wish you would NEVER hear again.

It's terrible when a music artist who you absolutely can't stand comes out with a song that you kinda love.

It's terrible when songs remind you of a time and place in your life.

It's terrible that once you've ***had the time of your life***...it's all downhill from there.

It's terrible that proms aren't as much fun as on TV.

It's terrible that dancing is never banned.

It's terrible that nobody ever spikes the punch.

It's terrible that nobody ever gets in a big fight.

It's terrible that the unlikely nerd never ends up with the prom king or queen.

It's terrible that a choreographed group dance montage never breaks out.

It's terrible when you see people rocking out while
they are driving.
It's terrible that our cars still run on gas.
It's terrible that we're all running on empty.
It's terrible when it is a "one-way" road, when you
have to go the other direction.
It's terrible that people can't follow directions.
It's terrible that I don't yield to oncoming traffic.
It's terrible when you don't yield to life's little signs.
It's terrible that life is heading right for us…and it's not
slowing down.

It's terrible that it's like people don't even know me.
It's terrible when "I just can't even."
It's terrible when you can't get even.
It's terrible when people say "yeah, no."
It's terrible that you know what they mean, "100%."

There are so many annoying little sayings that people use every day, "know what I mean?"

What are a couple of the irritating sayings that get on your last nerve?

____

____

It’s terrible that I don’t have a sexy accent.
It’s terrible that my sexy nightclub outfit involves comfy pj’s.
It’s terrible that I was ***raising my hands in the air, like I just don’t care***…long before the nightclub music told me to.
It’s terrible that we all don’t speak in rhyme.
It’s terrible when you are out of thyme.

It’s terrible when roses are red, and violets are blue….

It’s terrible when *everything* is terrible, the end.

Nobody's Business

It's terrible that I love gossip.
It's terrible that I can't keep a secret.
It's terrible that my own personal secrets are too juicy to keep to myself.
It's terrible that I don't think anyone could handle what I have kept to myself.

We all have hidden thoughts or dark secrets that we keep buried deep inside and likely will never share with anyone...ever. If you dare, write your deepest, darkest dirt on the page to the right and read it back to yourself.

You might want to get this off your chest and unload it on someone, but few, if any, might ever be worthy....So, right now, take a black ballpoint pen and scribble that page until it's COMPLETELY black, burying your secret back in that dark little corner of your soul.

→

It’s terrible that some things are better left alone.

Voodoo

It's terrible when you have a bad boss.
It's terrible when you've dated someone who thought they were the boss of you.
It's terrible when a person you thought was a "friend" shows up in your "recommended friends list."
It's terrible when the person in front of you on a plane fully reclines their seat.

Everything requires a little give-and-take; it's just sometimes when people are terrible, you want to give a little more.

Be creative and personalize the look of this voodoo doll so it looks like a terrible person. If you have a specific name, write it on the doll. Then go find something pointy like a pencil, ballpoint pen, or toothpick and Poke, Poke, Poke as many times as necessary. If you are feeling extra generous, poke it again.

It's terrible that you put so much energy into poking this page, but…it didn't make a bit of difference.

It’s terrible when your favorite stuffed animal is a better cuddler than anyone you know.

It’s terrible the things that my stuffed animal has seen.

It’s terrible when toys don’t come with batteries.

It’s terrible when you are out of batteries.

It’s terrible when your batteries die, but you’re not done playing.

It's terrible when your phone battery is down to 3%.
It's terrible when nobody has the same phone charger as you.
It's terrible when they charge you for a handling fee.
It's terrible when they charge you an automatic gratuity fee, and you paid a tip on top of it.
It's terrible when your credit card sees more action than you do.

RECEIPT
Entrée 1 $30
Entrée 2 $38
Appetizer $15
Dessert x2 $35
Drinks x5 $72
Total $190
Tip $40
20% Added Gratuity $38
Grand Total $268

EX's and OH's

It's terrible that it seems the hotter someone is, the crazier they are.
It's terrible that only crazy seems to swipe right on me.
It's terrible that I'm attracted to crazy.
It's terrible that I've come to realize that everyone is crazy.
It's terrible that dating drives me crazy.

There are reasons why your exes are now your exes, and some reasons are worse than others. If you had to count down your top 3 worst relationships in order from bad to worse to worst, what would that list of duds look like?

List those losers in the appropriate boxes on the next page, and then, in the banners below their name, write one word that best sums up why that person is your ex.

BAD
WORSE
WORST
It's terrible that I throw up in my mouth a little bit whenever I recall that my ex's lips have once touched my lips.

It's terrible when you run into your ex and they clearly look better off without you.

It's terrible when you are better off alone.

It's terrible when their new partner is ***super awesome*** and you wish you were friends.

It's terrible when you almost feel sorry for them, because YOU KNOW what is to come.

It's terrible when you take pride in knowing you were with them first.

It's terrible when you don't know how many people were before you.

It's terrible when you do find out how many there were before you.

It's terrible that everyone lies about their number.

It's terrible when there is no yin to your yang.
It's terrible when there is no peanut butter to your jelly.
It's terrible when there is no cheese to your macaroni.
It's terrible when there is no cheese.
It's terrible when there's no more dough.
It's terrible for anyone who comes between me and
my food.

Oil and Vinegar

It's terrible when they have a short fuse.
It's terrible when they have a big personality.
It's terrible when they can go all night.
It's terrible when they don't want to go.
It's terrible when that thing that attracted you to them now drives you insane.
It's terrible that opposites attract.

If you are oil, and they are vinegar, write down the qualities that you both have that just don't mix.

It’s terrible when you settle for the house salad.

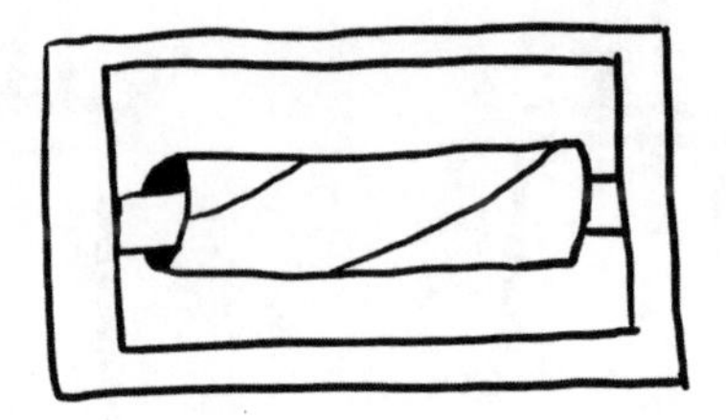

It's terrible when they bite their nails.
It's terrible when they leave their socks on the floor.
It's terrible when they leave their wet towel on the bed.
It's terrible when they don't clean their toilet before
having guests.
It's terrible when they don't replace the toilet paper.
It's terrible when they change the station.
It's terrible when they just talk about one thing.
It's terrible when they don't listen.

It’s terrible when they cough and don’t cover their mouth.
It’s terrible when they don’t wash their hands.
It’s terrible when they don’t recycle.
It’s terrible that nobody really knows what should be recycled.
It’s terrible when they don’t keep a secret.
It’s terrible when they don’t put it away.
It’s terrible when they keep saying that word wrong.
It’s terrible when they tell me how it’s going to end.

Short Fuse

It's terrible when they leave hair in the drain catch.
It's terrible when they eat the last one.
It's terrible when they talk with their mouth full.
It's terrible when they fill the dishwasher wrong.
It's terrible when I can hear them breathing.
It's terrible when they intentionally do things to annoy me.

It's terrible that we all have lots of piddly things that set us off too easily.

Label each firecracker with those little irritating things that one day just might make you crack. Within the M-80, put that one peeve that irks you the most.

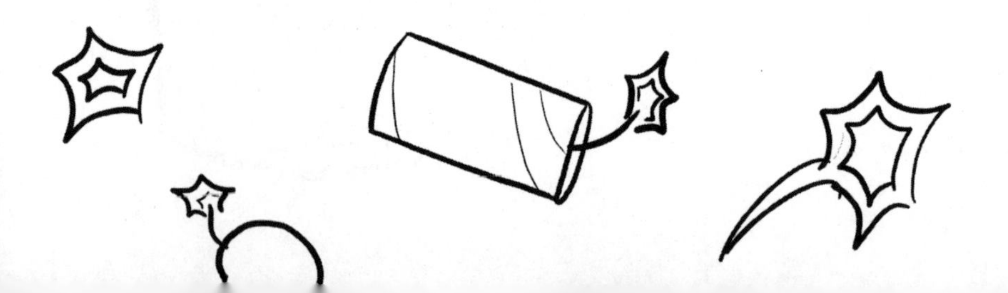

It's terrible when it's just one too many.

It’s terrible when you wake up on the wrong side
of the bed.
It’s terrible when you just can’t go back to bed.
It’s terrible when you go into the day knowing it’s going
to be…terrible.
It’s terrible when you say you just need to make it
through this week.
It’s terrible that you said that last week.

It's terrible when you have the worst day ever.

It's terrible when the next day tops it.

It’s terrible when you can’t help everyone.
It’s terrible when you can’t even help yourself.
It’s terrible when you don’t ask for help.
It’s terrible when people don’t offer to help.
It’s terrible that another helping…might help.
It’s terrible when you’ve had too much.
It’s terrible when you do too much.
It’s terrible not knowing when enough is enough.

It's terrible when there isn't enough filling in your doughnut.
It's terrible that there's never too much filling.

Recipe for Disaster

It's terrible when they won't share their secret family recipe.

It's terrible when your social feed is overfilled with crappy video recipes.

It's terrible when the videos make it look like you can make the dish in 15 seconds.

It's terrible when you are missing an ingredient.

It's terrible when you've never heard of some of the ingredients.

It's terrible when people try new recipes on you.

Though everything is terrible, some days are just simply worse than others. If you were to write a recipe for possibly the WORST DAY EVER, what would it include?

Worst Day Ever Recipe

1 large ____________

2-3 small ____________

1 can of ____________

1/2 bag of ____________

1 ____________ [finely chopped]

1 dash of ____________

Set the oven to 400°, then pour yourself a glass of wine. Combine all ingredients in a dish, and stick your head in the oven.

SPICES

It's terrible when it's not the onions that make you cry.

It’s terrible when your yolk breaks.
It’s terrible when it’s not over easy.
It’s terrible when the sunny side is not up.
It’s terrible that everything can’t be wrapped in bacon.
It’s terrible that I would be terrible in a rap battle.
It’s terrible when you get one shot, one opportunity.
It’s terrible when you’ve ***lost yourself***.

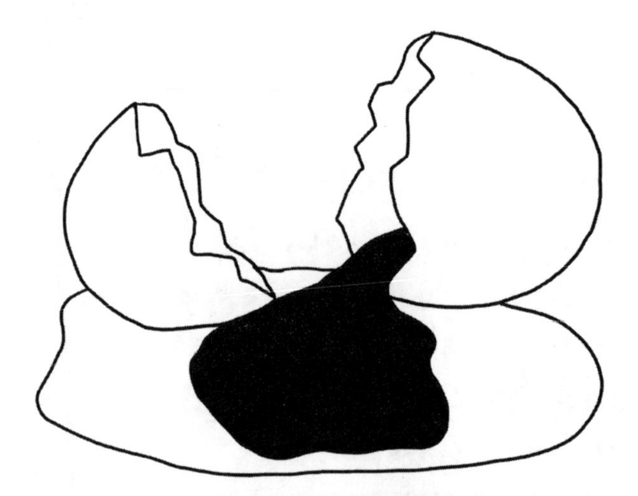

RU LE 1

RU LE 2

It's terrible when they make up their own rules.
It's terrible if you live by all the rules.

Rules are made to be broken. What are 3 rules that you break most frequently...or break intentionally, because they are dumb rules to begin with?

1. ____

2. ____

3. ____

It's terrible how you can't seem to manage to keep your car going straight…when a cop is behind you.
It's terrible if you feel guilty, even when you are not.
It's terrible if you don't feel guilty, when you are.

It’s terrible when it’s not what it looks like.
It’s terrible when it ***is*** what it looks like.
It’s terrible when it’s actually worse than what it looks like.

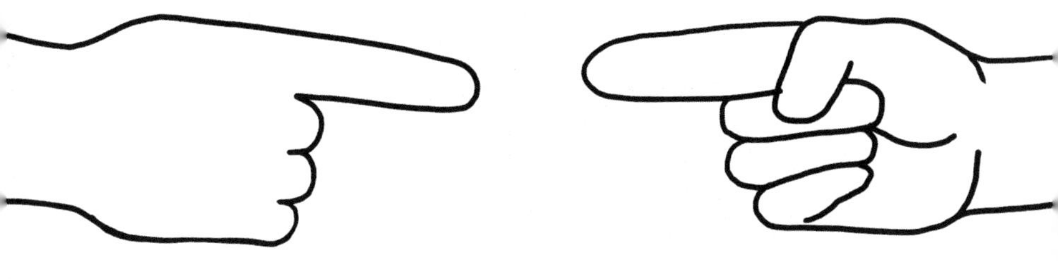

It’s terrible when you have nobody to blame.
It’s terrible when you do have somebody to blame.
It’s terrible that you would do it again.

Time Warp

It's terrible that our parents believed safety warnings and expiration dates were merely a suggestion.

It's terrible that our parents would intentionally undercook meat for juicy flavor.

It's terrible that our parents believed pesticides killed the germs and made you stronger.

It's terrible that I don't know how so many of us survived.

It's terrible that I do kinda believe a lot of that stuff made us stronger, and that kids today don't stand a chance.

It's terrible that a lot changes over the years, some for the better, but…***a lot*** for the worse.

When you think about it, there was quite a bit that was so much better when you were younger...and there were a whole bunch of things that you once enjoyed that don't exist anymore either!

Within the swirl of the lost past, list some things that are worse now...and in the boxes, list some things that you once enjoyed that no longer exist.

→

It's terrible that over time, one thing is consistent...the year you were born keeps moving further away.

Aged

It's terrible that when you are young, you can't wait to grow up.
It's terrible that when you are old, you wish time would slow down.
It's terrible when you are thirty, you do start slowing down.
It's terrible when you are forty, things start getting sore.
It's terrible when you are fifty, things start to break.
It's terrible when you are sixty, you need to fix things.
It's terrible that you are lucky to be seventy.
Anything past eighty is likely just terrible…but please let me know if you make it there!

Every age has its fair share of terrible things. What are the worst things about some of the terrible years you've experienced?

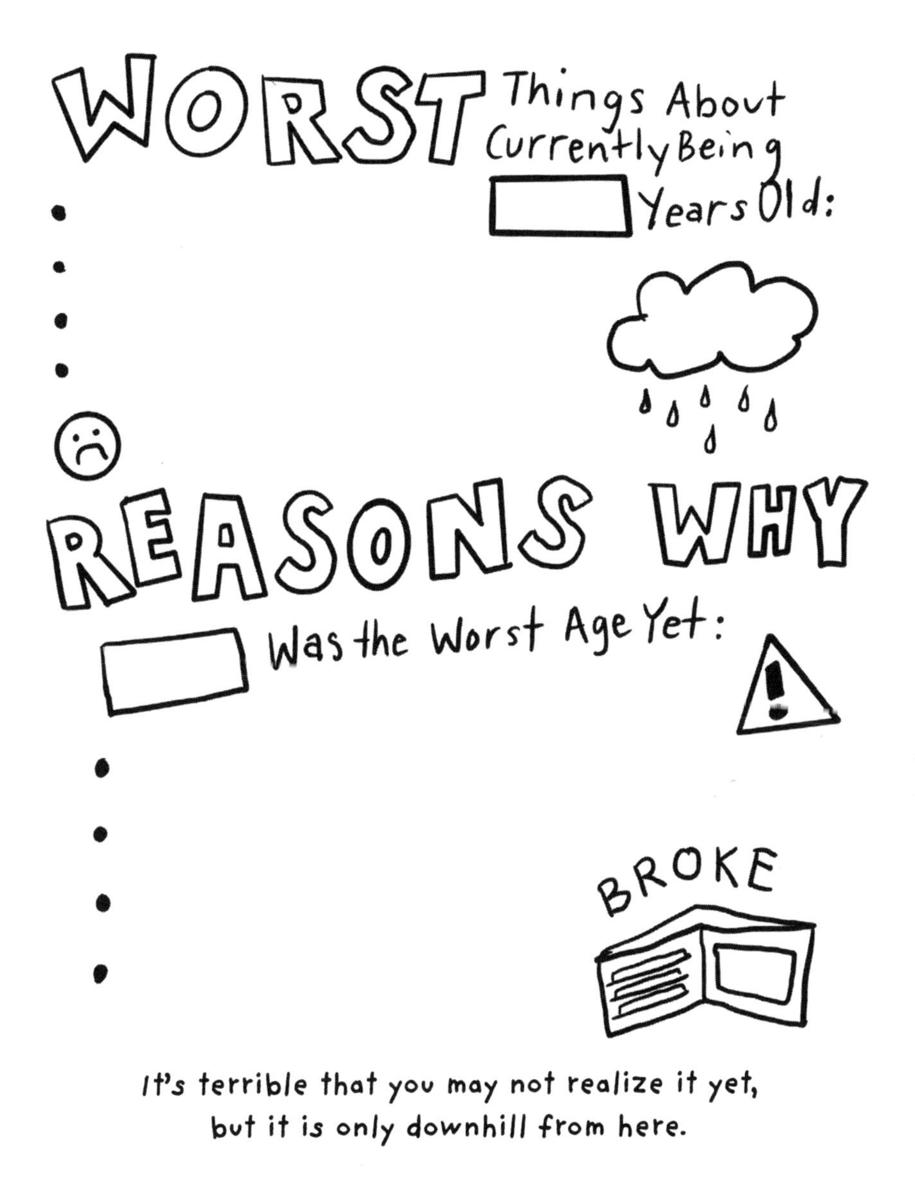
WORST Things About Currently Being
Years Old:
REASONS WHY
Was the Worst Age Yet:
BROKE
It's terrible that you may not realize it yet,
but it is only downhill from here.

It's terrible when you get too old to have posters on your wall.

It's terrible when they stop giving you lollipops at the bank.

It's terrible that they've yet to invent time travel…or so we think.

If you could travel back in time for your own selfish, terrible purpose, what 2 things would you do or try to change?

1. ______________________________

2. ______________________________

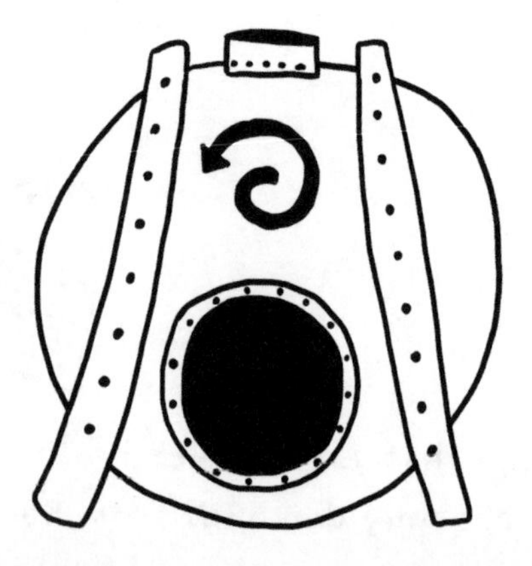

It's terrible that we're not prepared for a zombie outbreak.
It's terrible that I already grunt and moan through every day.
It's terrible that the government is likely to be the cause of a zombie apocalypse.
It's terrible that the government is already half full of zombies.

Bad Memories

It's terrible when you can't remember things.

It's terrible that memories can't be erased.

It's terrible that there are videos of some things that you wish there weren't.

It's terrible that once something is online, it's there for all time.

It's terrible when something seemed like a good idea at the time.

It's terrible that I can vividly remember the bad times.

There are plenty of terrible things that have left their mark on our lives. Since some of the specific unforgettable rotten memories made us who we are today, let's put them out there!

The class I struggled with the most
The first person who dumped me (or I dumped)
Terrible nickname they gave me
That sentimental thing you lost or no longer have
Where I got my first bee sting
First fight was with
It's terrible that what hasn't killed me...hasn't made me stronger.

Sharing Is Caring

It's terrible when people share their problems with me.
It's terrible that I have enough problems of my own.
It's terrible that no one cares about my problems.
It's terrible that I don't care about anyone else's problems.
It's terrible when their problems become my problems.

It's terrible that it's not enough that we stress about our own stuff, but that we also worry about other people's sh*t too. They say sharing is caring, but this is ridiculous. Label each poop emoji with other people's "sh*t" that weighs on you.

It's terrible when people think that their sh*t doesn't stink.
It's terrible that everyone's sh*t does stink.

It’s terrible when the things weighing on your mind keep you up at night.

It’s terrible when you lie there wide awake because you are worrying about how important getting a good night’s sleep is that night.

It’s terrible when you can’t sleep because you are afraid you will oversleep.

It’s terrible when you finally fall asleep right before you have to wake up.

It’s terrible when someone wakes you by asking, “Are you awake?”

It's terrible when they sleep on your side of the bed.
It's terrible when they have a side of the bed.
It's terrible when they take up the whole bed.
It's terrible when you drool in your sleep.
It's terrible that I'm pretty sure that I drool when I'm
dreaming of food.

It’s terrible when you have to wait to be seated.

It’s terrible when your server ***isn’t right with you***.

It’s terrible when the menu is coated in plastic.

It’s terrible when you can’t hear the specials at your end of the table.

It’s terrible when someone asks to repeat the specials… again.

It’s terrible when people custom order their dish.

It’s terrible when there is lipstick on your glass.

It's terrible when they don't check to make sure everything is okay.

It's terrible when they don't refill your drink.

It's terrible when they rush you to seat another table.

It's terrible when you want to sit at another table.

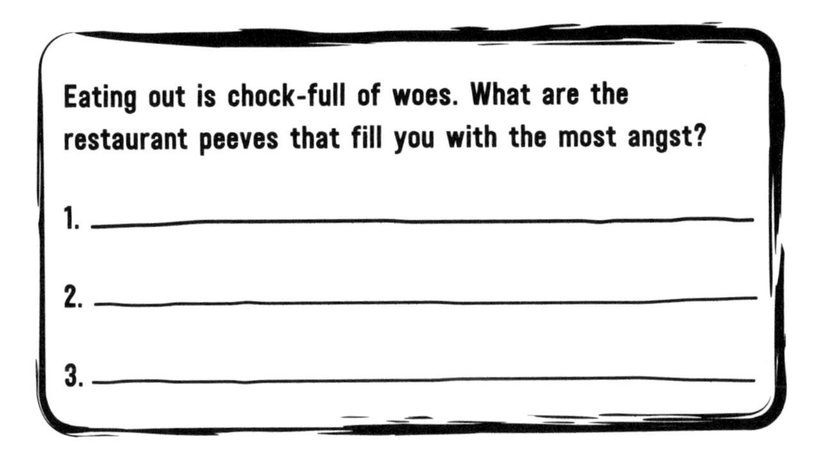

It's terrible when people order extra bread for their leftovers.

Things That Drive Me Nuts

It’s terrible that nice weather brings out mosquitoes… and keeps us trapped indoors.

It’s terrible that I want to stay home and have everyone come to me.

It’s terrible how many people go slow in the fast lane.

It’s terrible that we still follow people who post endless political views, food photos, or kid pics on social media.

It’s terrible when my video stream is interrupted by a commercial that is twice as long as the video itself.

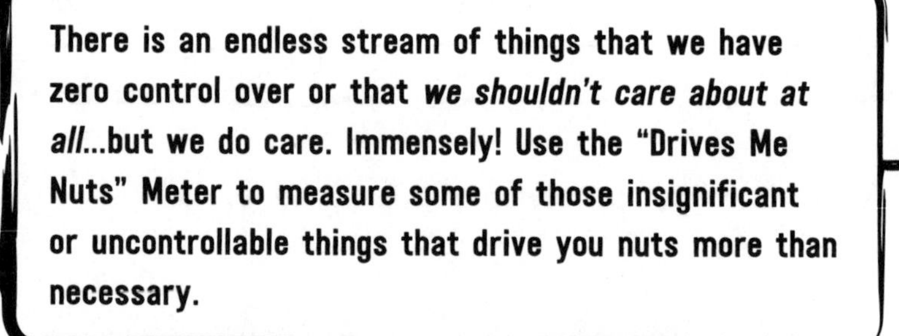

There is an endless stream of things that we have zero control over or that *we shouldn’t care about at all*...but we do care. Immensely! Use the “Drives Me Nuts” Meter to measure some of those insignificant or uncontrollable things that drive you nuts more than necessary.

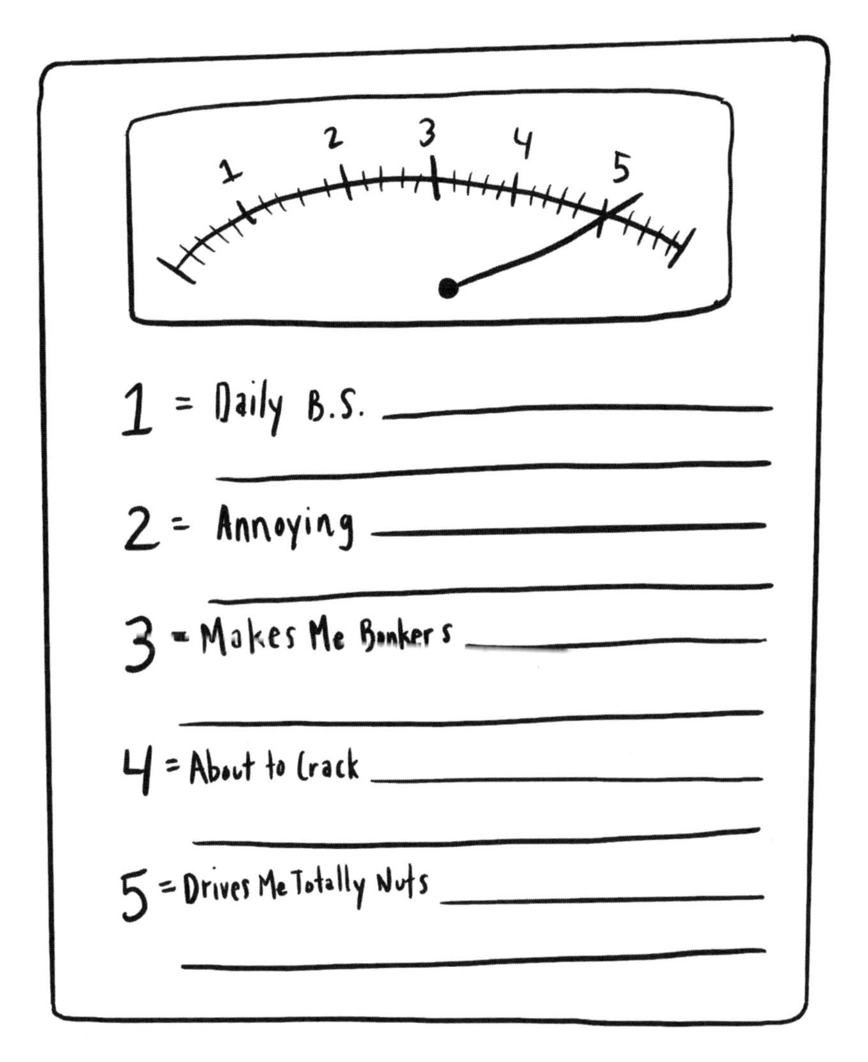

It’s terrible when the insanity of it all is off the charts.

Rotten Tomatoes

It's terrible when someone puts spoilers online.
It's terrible when they reboot movies that were perfect the first time around.
It's terrible that I still feel compelled to watch the movie reboots.
It's terrible how much time I've wasted watching movies over and over.

It's terrible that we know a bad movie when we see one… and we've seen our fair share.

In the movie marquee, showcase the absolute worst movies that you've wasted time watching. Highlight some of those with rotten tomatoes if you actually walked out of the theater or couldn't finish the movie because it was that bad.

It’s terrible that no matter how much we critique,
we’ll never be critics.

It's terrible when the DVR is out of space.

It's terrible when the DVR is filled with a bunch of things that nobody will ever watch.

It's terrible that there is now too much content available to watch.

It's terrible that award shows snub the movies we all like to see.

It's terrible that I'll never win a major award.

It's terrible that if you win one of those once-in-a-lifetime awards, they only give you 45 seconds to thank everyone.

It's terrible that I'd have plenty of time to spare.

It’s terrible when people kick your chair at the movies.
It’s terrible when people bring their crying kids to late-night movies.
It’s terrible when people act like kids at the movies and ruin your theater experience.
It’s terrible when it’s cheaper to buy a movie than to see it in the theater.
It’s terrible when you buy a movie and only watch it once.
It’s terrible that I’ve bought movies and have never watched them.

It's terrible when you feel like you are being watched.
It's terrible that there are cameras everywhere.
It's terrible that you can no longer do anything stupid,
unless you want it on "film."
It's terrible that we still use the old words when they're
no longer relevant.

It’s terrible that we’ve reached the future.
It’s terrible that cars still aren’t flying.
It’ll be terrible when cars are able to fly.

Big Brother

It's terrible when you see an ad on your phone for something you were JUST talking about.
It's terrible when my phone overhears someone else's conversation about adult diapers.
It's terrible that my phone knows where I am and can predict where I'm going.
It's terrible that I don't even know where I'm heading.

It's terrible that George Orwell's sci-fi novel *1984* predicted that Big Brother would someday be watching.
It's terrible that, wherever you go, there is a technology that is always watching and listening.

Now that you know you are always being watched, what are the worst things that Big Brother has probably seen you do or heard you say?

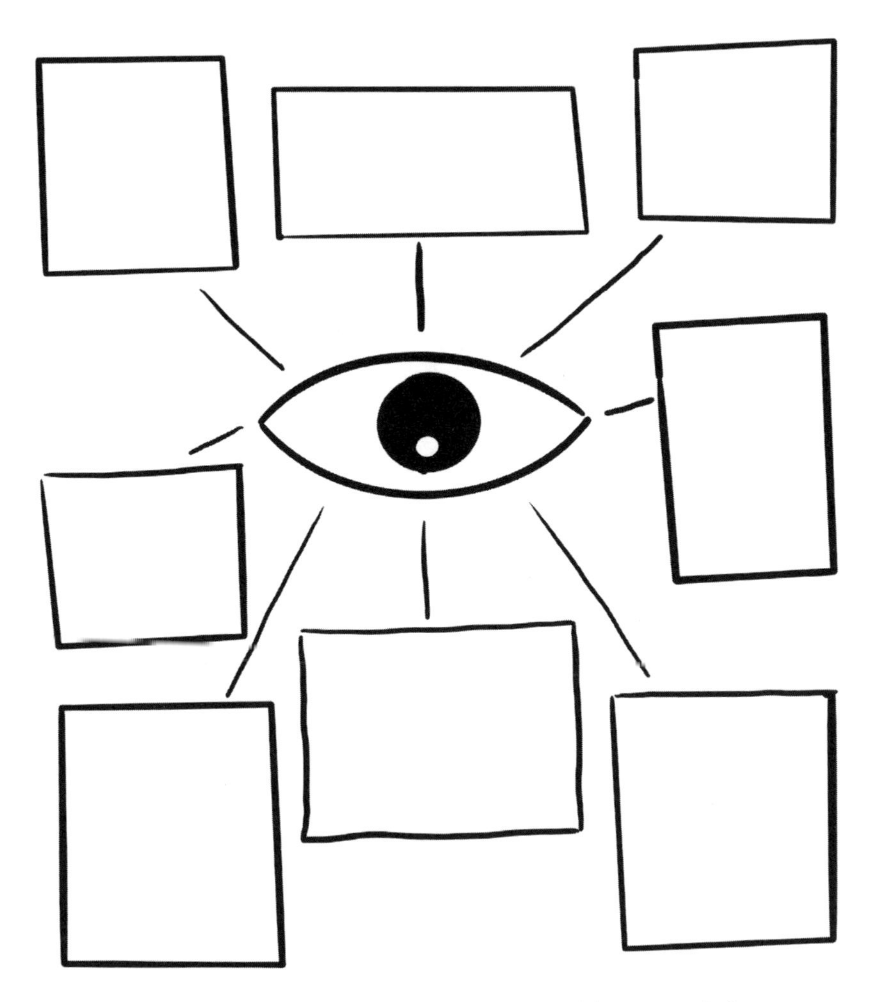

It’s terrible if you think they are not watching you right now. It’s terrible that we’ve clicked on the disclaimers agreeing to let this happen.

It's terrible how much I ♥ my bathrobe.

It's terrible that my significant other now only sees me in comfy, sloppy house clothes.

It's terrible that I've reached the point where I'm actually okay going out in those clothes.

It's terrible when I run into someone unexpected while I'm dressed like a slob.

It's terrible that I've traded sexy underwear for comfy underwear.

It's terrible that I have more underwear on my bedroom floor than in my drawer.

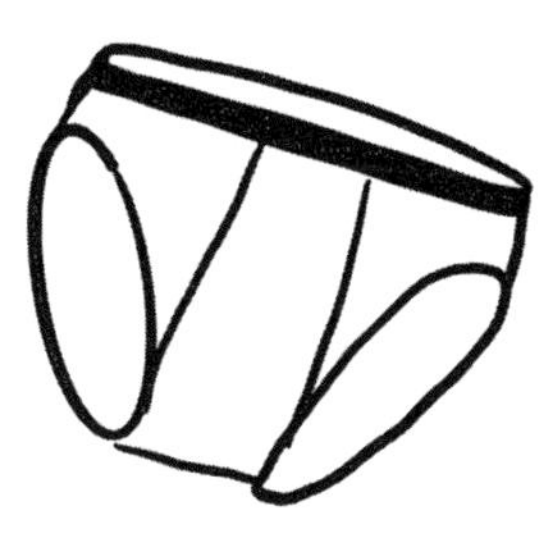

It’s terrible that I prefer cuddling with my pet.
It’s terrible that my significant other’s new endearing
pet name for me is “stinky.”
It’s terrible that few can truly handle the real me.

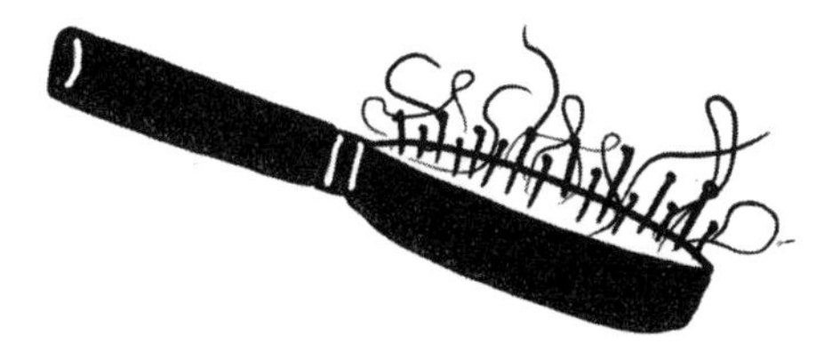

SO Selfish!

It's terrible how much I enjoy sleep.
It's terrible that I don't get enough of it.
It's terrible that I don't know where my day goes.
It's terrible that no matter how hard I try…I'm always late.
It's terrible how annoyed I get when other people make me late.
It's terrible that sometimes I take my time replying to texts.
It's terrible that I want them to respond to my text NOW.
It's terrible that my priorities may be a little selfish.
It's terrible when people put their priorities ahead of mine.

People can be so self-centered, putting themselves as the most important thing, no matter who it affects. What are the selfish things that people do that just make your head explode?!

It's terrible when someone eats
one of your french fries.

It's terrible that I could never pull off some of the hairstyles that I like.

It's terrible when you forget that hair just grows back.

It's terrible that hair sometimes doesn't grow back.

It's terrible when you just want to stay under the radar.

It's terrible that you wish you could still play hide-and-seek…and just hide.

It's terrible when you were tagged "it" as a kid.

It's terrible if you were never the "it" kid.

It's terrible when people just watch the Super Bowl for the commercials.

It's terrible when you pretend to like sports and people ask you sports questions.

It's terrible when the closest people get to being athletic is playing in fantasy sports leagues.

It's terrible that in my fantasies, I wanted to be an Olympian.

It's terrible that I've considered taking up curling to make the dream come true.

It's terrible that I likely won't break any records…but curling is on ice, so there's a good chance something might get broken.

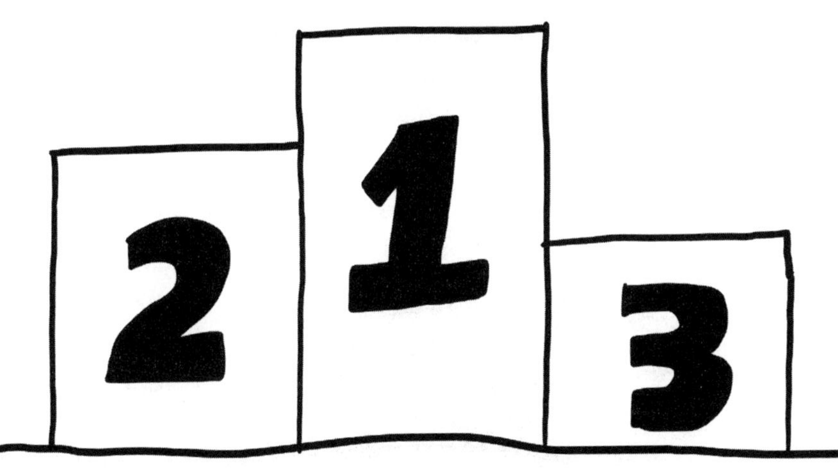

Broken

It's terrible that we usually only get stung by bees
while we're playing.
It's terrible that bees get stepped on while they're working.
It's terrible that so do I.
It's terrible when you get bit by a dog for trying to pet it.
It's terrible when you bite into a perfect piece of fruit…and
find that it is terribly bruised.
It's terrible that if I drop a piece of fruit at the market, I'll
put it back and get a fresh one.

We've all been banged up before, one way or another. Draw lines pointing to the skeleton and document all the parts of you that have been hurt or broken in your entire lifetime.

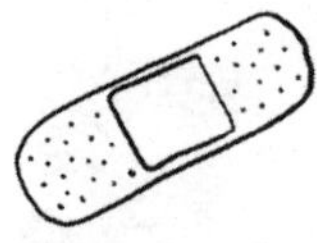

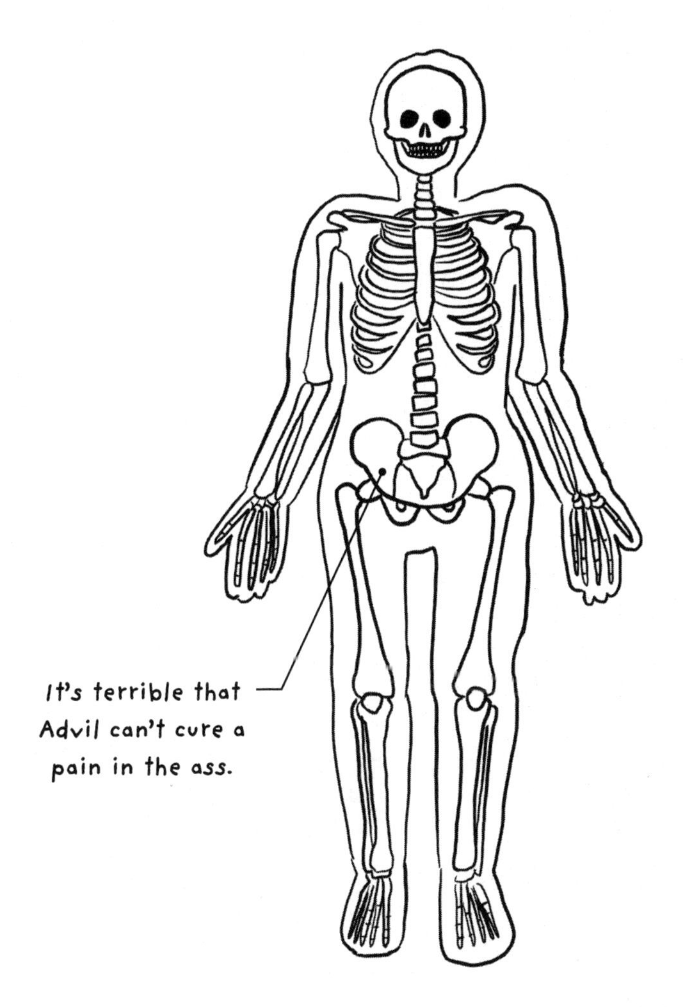

It's terrible that some don't realize that underneath it all,
we are the same.
It's terrible to be like everyone else.

It's terrible when you see a car broken down on the side of the road.

It's terrible that I never stop to help people who are broken down.

It's terrible that I break down nearly every day.

It's terrible that karma is a b*tch.

It's terrible if something broke you a long time ago.

It's terrible if you can't remember how long it's been since you've smiled.

It's terrible if you don't even try to smile for pictures anymore.
It's terrible that there are people who never smile in pictures.
It's terrible that we know people who shouldn't smile in pictures.
It's terrible when you have to put on a fake smile.
It's terrible when people are fake.
It's terrible when you want to wipe that antagonizing grin off someone's face.

Face the Facts

It's terrible when you find an empty toilet paper roll on the holder…and the second one sitting on top of it is 98% gone.

It's terrible when you have to buy something you don't need…because you were 2 cents away from free shipping.

It's terrible when your day is 100% ruined due to one person.

It's terrible when facial recognition only picks up your scowling face.

It's terrible when you can't find the perfect emoji to suit your mood.

Face it, when surrounded by so many terrible things, it shows on our face. Put a corresponding percentage of time that best reflects the moods that people see on your face most of the time.

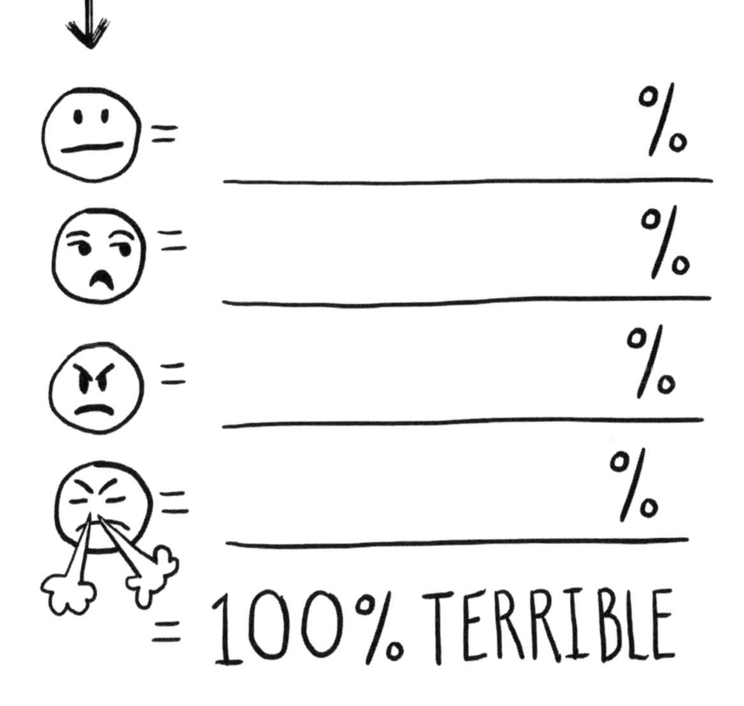

It's terrible when you haven't used those muscles in a while…and it hurts to smile.

It’s terrible when someone tells you the odds.
It’s terrible when the odds are not in your favor.
It’s terrible when you are under pressure.
It’s terrible when you are under construction.

It's terrible when you are under suspicion.
It's terrible when you are going under.
It's terrible when you are under the gun.
It's terrible if you are going under the knife.
It's terrible when you are under attack.
It's terrible that under no circumstances does any of this
matter when you are 6 feet underground

Boogeyman

It's terrible when you see someone picking their nose.
It's terrible when you have to reach for something under your bed.
It's terrible what lurks in my closet at night.
It's terrible that I can't sleep if I know my closet door is even slightly cracked open.

People have their own horrid thoughts of what the boogeyman who lurks in their closet looks like...and each vision is vastly different. Using your best artistic skills, show us what your boogeyman looks like.

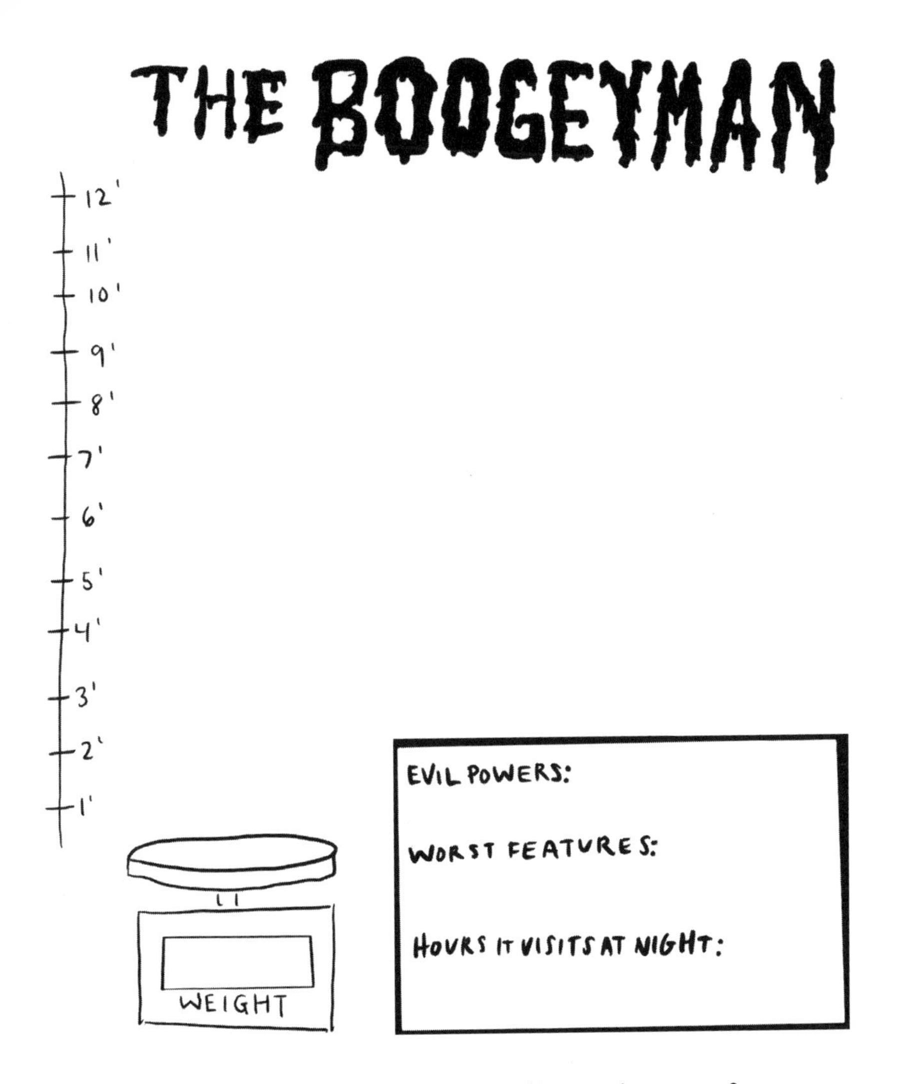

It's terrible when your imagination gets away from you.

It's terrible that we never see anyone smiling in the morning.

It's terrible when you do see someone smiling in the morning.

It's terrible that, if smiles and laughter are infectious, I'm not sure if I want to catch them.

It's terrible that they needed to make pharmaceuticals that will make you happy.

It's terrible that they read all those drug side effects in an acceptable happy voice.

It's terrible when the drug side effects are worse than the problem.

It's terrible when you need to take other drugs to fix the side effects.

It's terrible that there are never any ***good*** side effects.

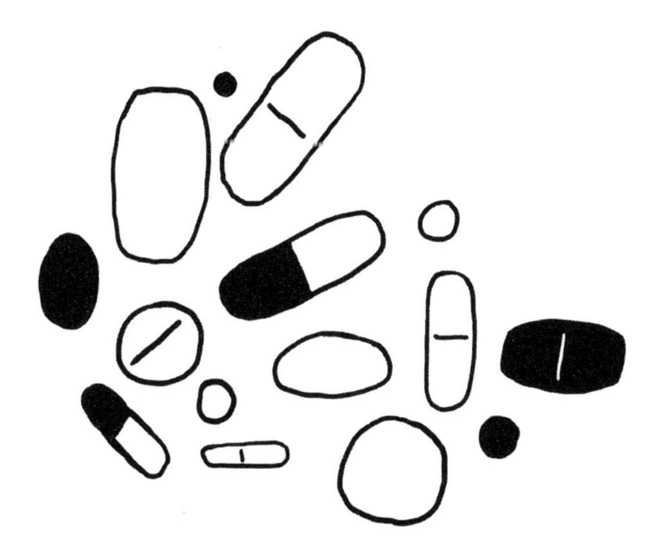

Side Effects

It's terrible that we can't stay young forever.
It's terrible when you find your first gray hair.
It's terrible when you find your first wrinkle.
It's terrible that life has so many wrinkles.

It's terrible that we deal with so much stress.
It's terrible that stress prematurely ages you.
It's terrible that each tired bag under your eye, each hair that has fallen out, and your high blood pressure are all signs of aging…and too much stress.

Pinpoint the causes of your stress by writing in who or what is to blame for each area affected.

It's terrible that everything gets blamed on me.
It's terrible that I usually had something to do with it.

It's terrible when it's faster to go in than using the drive-through lane.

It's terrible when you have to pull aside to wait for your fast food.

It's terrible when you get home and your takeout order is missing something.

It's terrible how much you'll pay for something you could have easily done at home…for free.

It's terrible when people expect things for free.

It's terrible that if it's free, I'll take it whether I need it or not.

It's terrible that when it's "sugar-free," it's replaced with chemicals instead.

It's terrible that they offer the option to buy a diet soda with fast food.

It's terrible when you can't even pronounce the scientific artificial ingredients in your food.

It's terrible that no matter how they rename fake sugar to sound natural…you can always taste that awful flavor.

It's terrible that I'm more bitter than ever.

It’s terrible that Oreos are vegan.
It’s terrible that Oreos went and put Mega Stuf crème on the inside.
It’s terrible that I could eat a whole pack of Oreos in one sitting.
It’s terrible that I have eaten a whole pack of Oreos in one sitting.
It’s terrible when too much of a good thing makes it less desirable.

It's terrible when you can't eat just one.

It's terrible that I'll never be as fit as I want to be.

It's terrible that I always have room to fit one more cookie in my mouth.

What are 2 terribly wonderful things that you can't stop eating once you start?

1. ______________________________

2. ______________________________

It's terrible when there are fit people at the gym.

It's terrible when you start sweating just thinking about working out.

It's terrible when that sweaty guy doesn't wipe down the gym equipment.

It's terrible how many excuses we use to not work out.

It's terrible when you have to rush eating.

It's terrible when you use a smaller plate to fool yourself
that your plate is full.

It's terrible when you then go back for seconds.

It's terrible when there are no leftovers.

It's terrible when a restaurant doesn't take reservations.

It's terrible when you made but didn't need a reservation.

It's terrible when a restaurant doesn't hold your reservation.

It's terrible when you don't understand how a business is still in business.

It's terrible when you really want to like a NEW business… but it's just awful.

It's terrible when their bathroom is near where people can hear you doing your business.

It's terrible that most new businesses go down the tubes.

It's terrible when someone is all up in your business.

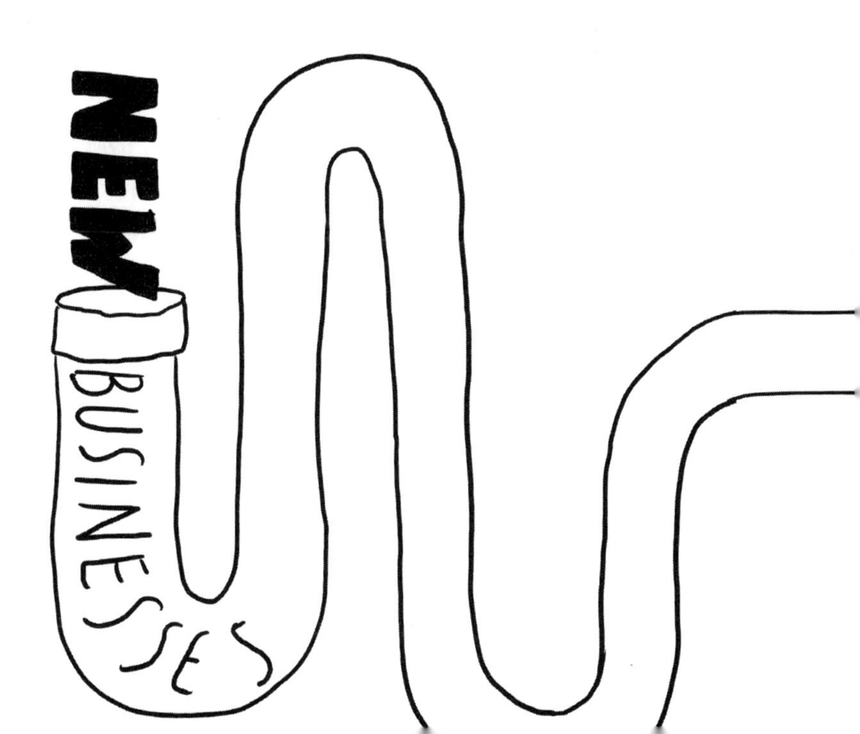

Bad Business

It's terrible when a business has a bad website.
It's terrible when a business doesn't return your calls.
It's terrible when they are in the service industry and their service s*cks.
It's terrible that ANYBODY can now rate a business.

It takes a lot to earn our business, but it doesn't take much to p*ss us off and alienate us from ever spending our money with them ever again. In the following online reviews, write down the businesses that you've cut off...and, more importantly, why.

BAD REVIEWS

Worst Businesses Ever:

It's terrible when you want to cut off a business, but there is one thing you like or really need them for.

It’s terrible when you are missing a button.
It’s terrible when your zipper gets stuck.
It’s terrible when your shoelace breaks.
It’s terrible when you get the boot.
It’s terrible when you shoot yourself in your foot.
It’s terrible when you drag your feet.

It’s terrible that some people don’t realize that they have ugly feet.

It’s terrible when you put your foot in your mouth.

It’s terrible when you have to get your feet wet.

It’s terrible when someone gives you a “dead-fish” handshake.

It’s terrible when you are all nervous and clammy on a first date, and they want to hold hands.

It’s terrible when your friends all thought it…but they didn’t warn you to run away.

It’s terrible when there is no way out.

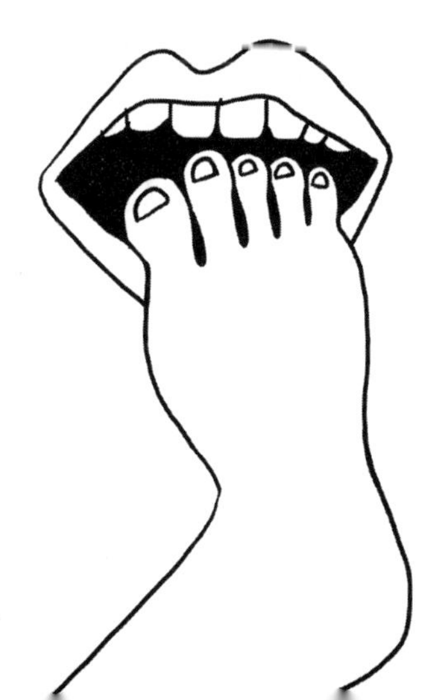

It's terrible when you feel cooped up.
It's terrible when you need to break out.
It's terrible when you are unable to spread your wings.
It's terrible when you are spread too thin.
It's terrible when they spread the cream cheese too thin.
It's terrible that it always comes back to food.

It's terrible when someone double-dips.
It's terrible when kids are allowed to dip themselves.
It's terrible when the person serving licks food off
their fingers.
It's terrible when your food touches.
It's terrible when people don't feel food on their face.
It's terrible when you lose your appetite.
It's terrible that it takes a lot for me to lose my appetite.

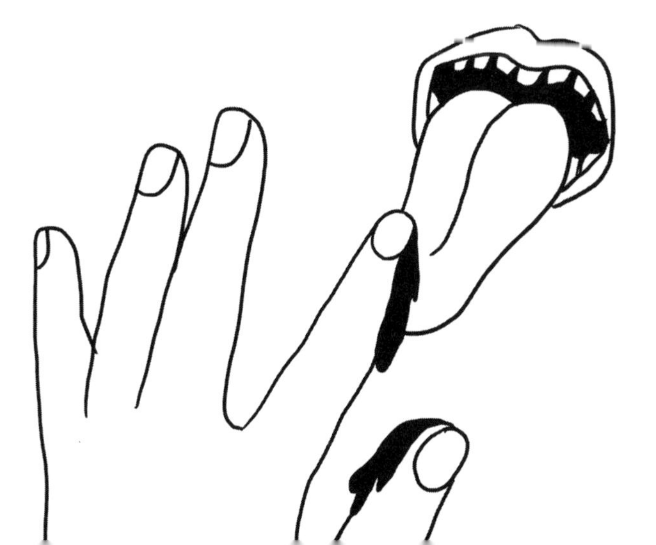

Foodie

It's terrible how much I like food.
It's terrible that pizza and tacos are not daily recommended food groups.
It's terrible that reheated pizza never tastes the same.
It's terrible that I only crave and enjoy things that aren't good for me.
It's terrible that I don't eat to live, but instead…I live to eat.

It's terrible that we all know what food we should and shouldn't eat, but we are all wired to satisfy our indulgences.

If you could rewrite the 5 food groups into those terribly wonderful things that you just can't resist and wish you could live on every day, what would that chart look like?

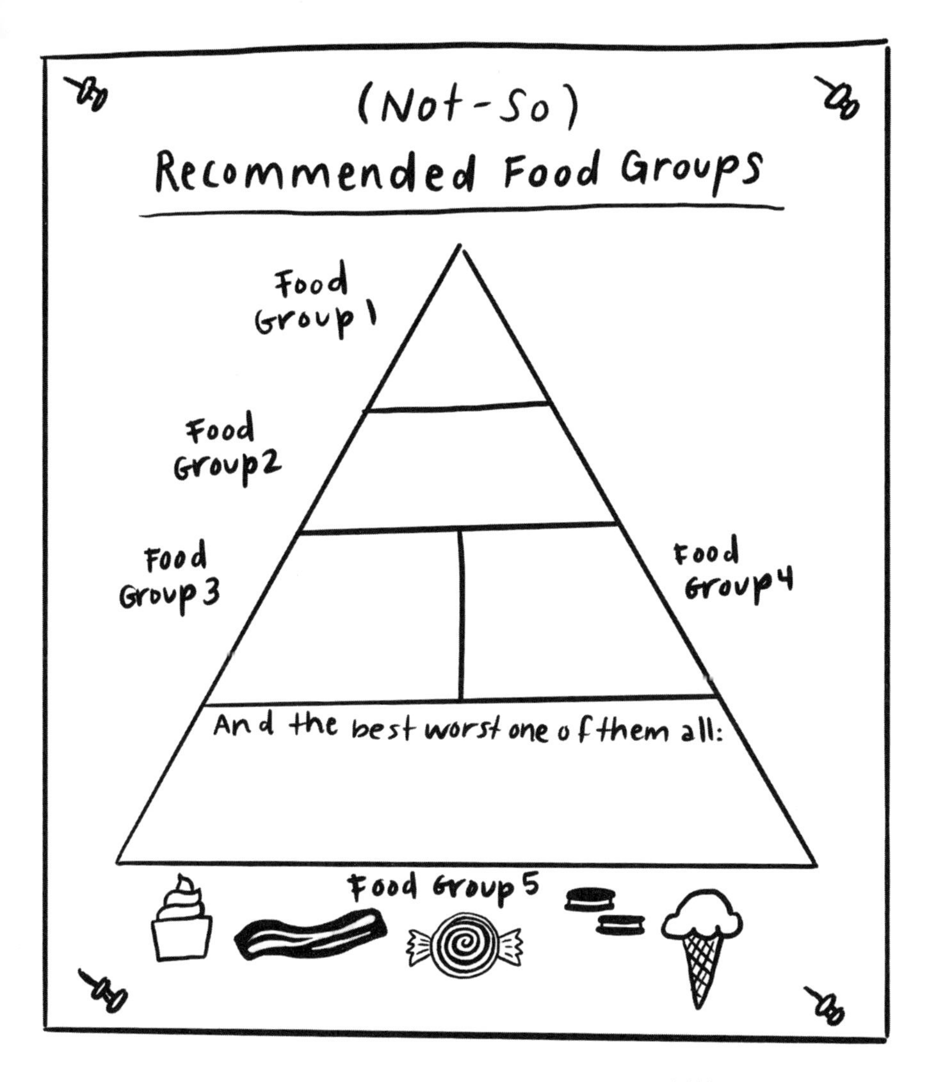

It's terrible when what you love tries to kill you.

It’s terrible that menus now list the calories.

It’s terrible that sugar substitutes are worse for you than sugar.

It’s terrible that my body can’t process processed food.

It’s terrible that processed cheese both melts and tastes
better than real cheese.
It’s terrible that cheese makes food that is bad for you taste
even better.
It’s terrible that my favorite cheese flavor is the artificial
one they use for Cheez-Its.
It’s terrible when food flavors that could be real are done
artificially.
It’s terrible how much I spoil myself with food that
doesn’t spoil.

Deserted

It's terrible that when they bring around the dessert tray, you want it all.
It's terrible when you don't save room for dessert…then eat it anyway.
It's terrible when you are the only one who orders dessert, but then everyone gets a spoon.
It's terrible when you're eating out and others shortchange or desert you before the bill comes.

It's terrible that being stranded on a deserted island, away from everyone…doesn't sound so terrible.

With our luck, if stranded on a deserted island, we'd get stuck with that one person who we loathe the most in this world. Alive or dead, someone you know or someone famous, who is the LAST person in the world that you would ever want to be stranded with alone...and why would you not want to be stranded with them?

→

It's terrible that you can always count on two things: (1) a worst-case scenario, and (2) that worst-case scenario actually happening.

It's terrible when you get seasick.
It's terrible when you are surrounded by sick people.
It's terrible when things are read the wrong way.
It's terrible that having cake by the ocean means something naughty.
It's terrible that I'd like to have my cake and eat it too.
It's terrible that I'd like to have your cake too.

It’s terrible when their food doesn’t taste like your mom’s.
It’s terrible when you realize that your mom wasn’t a
great cook.
It’s terrible when you turn into your parents.
It’s terrible that our parents had to put up with us.
It’s terrible that we put up with people who think they
know more than scientists.
It’s terrible when other people leave a mess for you to
clean up.

It's terrible that just when you finish dusting, you
need to dust again.
It's terrible when you can't recall the last time
you vacuumed.
It's terrible when someone walks across
your fresh carpet vacuum lines.
It's terrible when you break your own
"no eating on the new couch" rule.
It's terrible that cleaning takes a
whole day.
It's terrible if you buy things
in strategic colors so you
won't see that they
are dirty.

It's terrible when the garbage is full, but you keep
piling it in to avoid taking it out.
It's terrible that haste makes waste.
It's terrible when an animal spreads your garbage
across the lawn.
It's terrible when your neighbors see what you throw out.
It's terrible when you don't like your neighbors.
It's terrible when your neighbors don't like you.
It's terrible if your neighbor's yard is meticulously
groomed.
It's terrible if your neighbor's yard is an overgrown dump.
It's terrible that we are happiest with the status quo.

Reality Check

It's terrible that my five-year plan has been my five-year plan for ten years.

It's terrible that my goals may be a tad unrealistic.

It's terrible when other people accomplish their goals before me.

It's terrible that we don't know what the future holds.

It's terrible that I put too much faith in fortune-tellers.

Sometimes we know the hard truth, but we need to ask anyway. Ask the Magic 8-Ball a yes or no question...and then close your eyes and point to the page to see what answer you get! →

It's terrible when your Magic 8-Ball gives up on you too.

It's terrible when the outlook does not look good. It's terrible when you have to be the lookout. It's terrible when your crew is only around for the goodtimes. It's terrible when people go overboard. It's terrible when your life is just on autopilot. It's terrible when your life can't be on a relaxing cruise control. It's terrible when that ship has sailed.

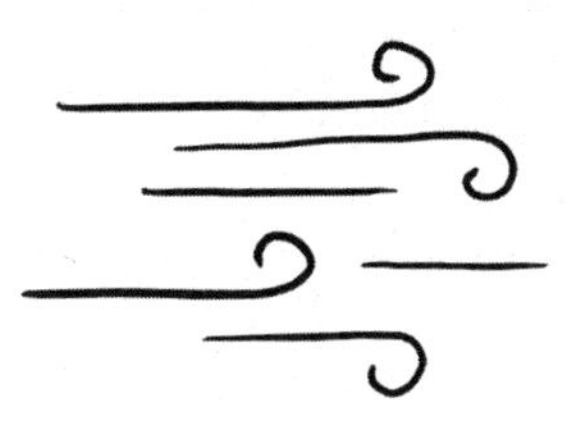

It's terrible when the wind is not at your back.
It's terrible when you don't know where you are going to wind up.
It's terrible when they get you all wound up.
It's terrible when you get wounded along the way.
It's terrible that the English language really likes to mess with people.
It's terrible that sub, submarine, hoagie, hero, po'boy, grinder, torpedo, and sandwich all mean the same exact thing.
It's terrible when they all sound delicious and you can't decide.

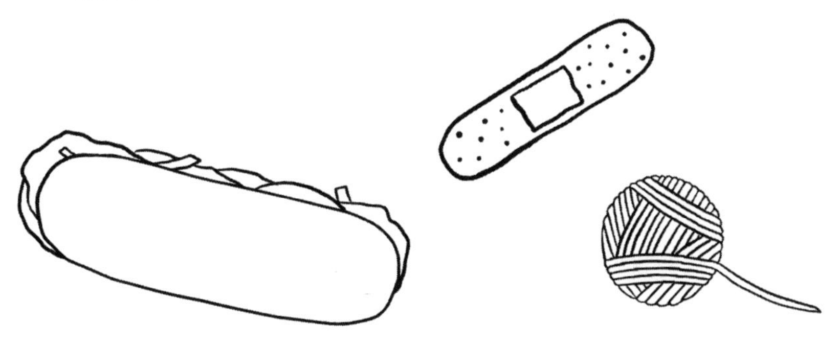

This or That

It's terrible when you are surrounded by indecisive people.
It's terrible when people answer a question with a question.
It's terrible when you finally make a decision for someone, and they say no to that.
It's terrible when people have strong opinions.
It's terrible when others don't understand that you are always right.

When it comes to having a choice between one thing or another, you usually base your decision on "which is the better option?" But what if both options are terrible?

Let's learn what is worse to you by answering these quick terrible questions:

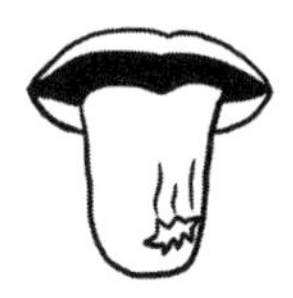

CIRCLE ONE:

Burn your tongue OR Bite your lip

Lost item OR Broken item

Hangnail OR Brush burn

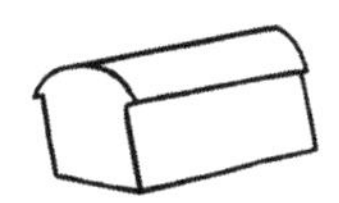

Give up sweets OR Give up breads

Stranger's hair in mouthful of food OR
Bandage in dish you've been eating

Mosquito bite OR Bird poop on the head

Stubbed toe OR Splinter

Allergic to alcohol OR Allergic to caffeine

Step in dog poop barefoot OR Step in cat puke barefoot

It's terrible when it's a lose-lose situation.

It's terrible when someone asks to borrow a pen...and you never see it again.

It's terrible when someone asks to borrow a tissue.

It's terrible when you sniff your dirty clothes to see if you can wear them one more time.

It's terrible when you have that first sign of a cold...and know the next two weeks are doomed.

It's terrible when everyone has the flu shot but you.

It's terrible when people come in to work sick.

It's terrible when you are Flu Ground Zero for all your friends and family.

People are so dirty, spreading germs everywhere. If you were to do a petri dish test, what is probably the dirtiest, germiest thing you touch during the day?

____

____

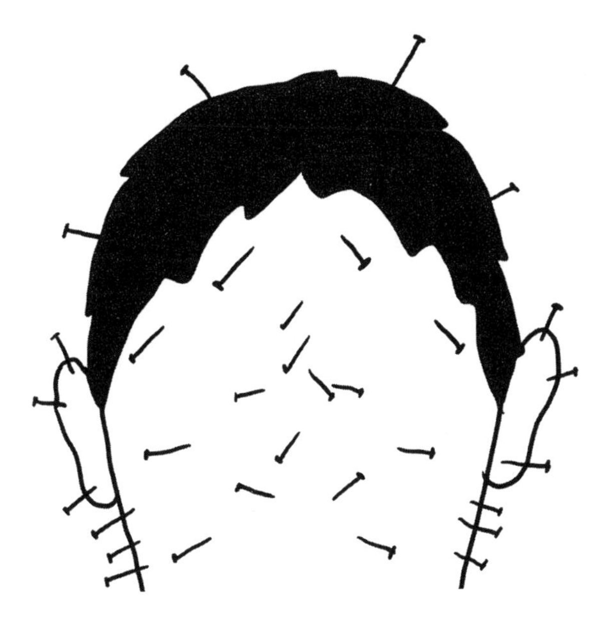

It's terrible that massages require strangers touching you.
It's terrible that acupuncture involves needles.
It's terrible that hot tubs are cesspools of germs.
It's terrible when you don't have the time or money for
a vacation.
It's terrible that shopping therapy causes other headaches.
It's terrible when you don't have the patience for yoga.
It's terrible that you can't drink all day.

It’s terrible when nothing can help relieve your stress.
It’s terrible when people complain about everything.
It’s terrible when there is no escape.
It’s terrible when having to escape from an escape room is considered entertainment.

It's terrible when you have no clue.
It's terrible when people make it look easy.
It's terrible when life is easier for others.
It's terrible when a dark little rain cloud follows you around.
It's terrible when there is a 100% chance of showers.
It's terrible when everyone else would rather stay dry.
It's terrible when you forget to put clothes in the dryer.

To-Do List

It's terrible that the dryer doesn't work as fast as the washer.
It's terrible when you need to buy new underwear.
It's terrible when you have to schedule a haircut.
It's terrible when your bills aren't auto-paid.
It's terrible when you need to go buy a thank-you card.

It's terrible that there is always something that has to be done...and those things take away from any fun we might even be able to muster up. What are the most annoying chores or activities that you have to do but hate doing?

It's terrible when your to-do list just keeps getting longer.

It's terrible that we don't stop to watch the sunset.

It's terrible that Earth will make another trip around the sun before we know it.

It's terrible that you can't click reboot on your day.

It's terrible that it's darkest before dawn.

It's terrible that the moon makes people crazier than they already are.

It's terrible that the sun doesn't shine in the shade.

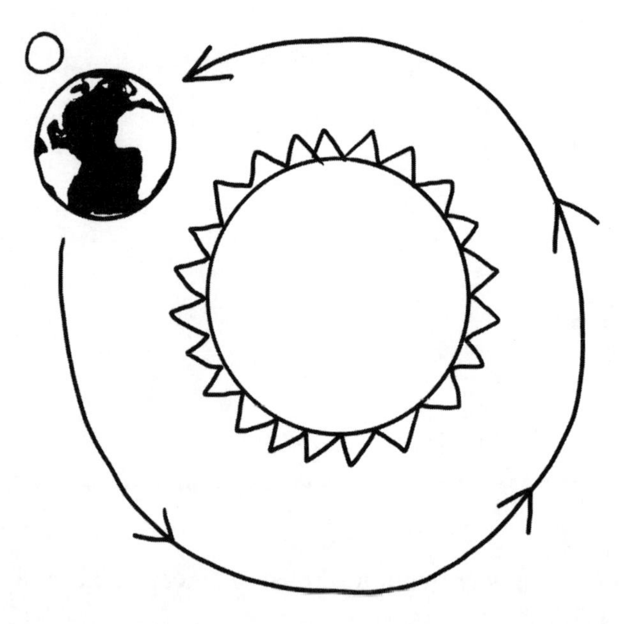

It's terrible that 99% of all sunglasses look ridiculous
on me.
It's terrible when you lose that one pair of sunglasses
that did work on you.
It's terrible when the sunglasses that do work on you are
not prescription…and you can't see a thing.
It's terrible the pains we go through to look good.
It's terrible when you forget your sunglasses.
It's terrible when the future's not looking so bright.

It's terrible that stores have back-to-school ads just when summer is getting good.

It's terrible when you catch that back-to-school smell in the air at the end of summer.

It's terrible when you need a whole summer off to catch up on everything.

It's terrible when you look back and realize all the summers off you've wasted.

It's terrible that you would do anything to waste a summer off now.

We all had that one teacher who we couldn't stand for one reason or another. Who was or is it for you?

___

It's terrible when all the studying in the world isn't going to help.

It's terrible when there is more homework than you can do in a single day.

It's terrible when you can't wait to get out of school and get into the real world.

It's terrible that when you are in the real world, you wish you could go back to school.

It's terrible that school doesn't better prepare you for life.
It's terrible that we don't live every day.
It's terrible that school doesn't prepare you for relationships.
It's terrible that after several relationships, I haven't learned a thing.
It's terrible that life doesn't prepare you for life.

It's terrible when you are in the freshman class.
It's terrible when they classify you.
It's terrible when you have no class.
It's terrible when we don't learn our lesson.
It's terrible when you walk past and wonder what
the people who are in first class do.
It's terrible when you have high-class interests on
a low-class budget.

It’s terrible that my budget is so tight.
It’s terrible that I don’t stretch more.
It’s terrible that the average body is 70% water…but mine is 25% coffee, 25% booze, and 50% p*ss and vinegar.
It’s terrible that I should eat more salad.

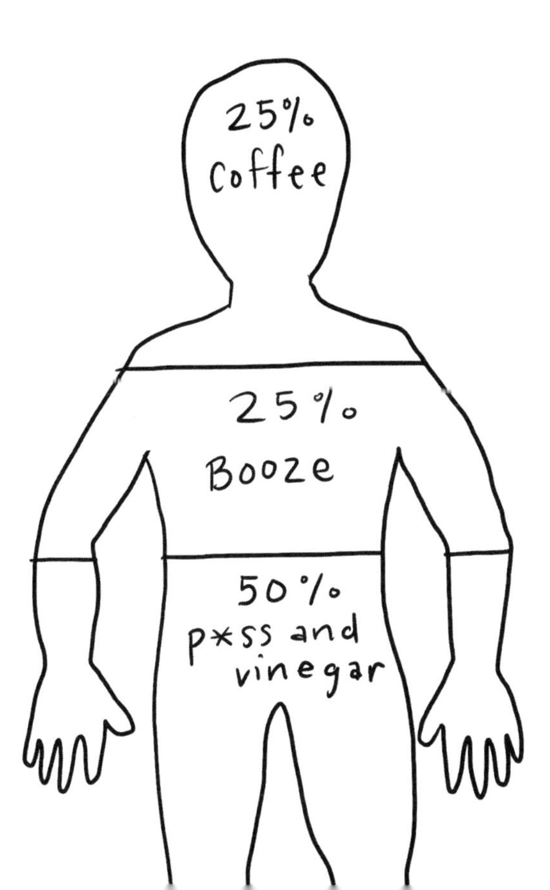

Hall Pass

It's terrible that people are so engrossed in celebrities.
It's terrible when you don't know half the celebrities or
why they are "famous."
It's terrible that I'll never be famous.
It's terrible that I'll never hobnob with anyone famous.

In a relationship, hall passes are lists of celebrities you would be allowed to "cheat with" if the opportunity should ever come up. In top 5 celeb order, write out your hall pass list. (As if it would ever happen.)

It’s terrible that, even though the chance is extremely limited, we still have hope.

It's terrible that news has lost all of its integrity.

It's terrible that there is more news on "celebrities" than real news.

It's terrible that the only news left worth watching is the weather...and everyone has an app for that.

It's terrible when weathercasters exaggerate how bad the weather is when standing out in a major storm.

It's terrible when people don't sugarcoat bad news.

It's terrible when you have to be the bearer of bad news.
It's terrible when you can't bear any more bad news.
It's terrible when something is too good to be true.
It's terrible when someone asks, "Do you want the good news or the bad news?"
It's terrible that it's never just good news.
It's terrible that no matter how bad something is, it could always be worse.

It's terrible that cable TV costs SO much, and the price keeps going up every year.
It's terrible that no single TV streaming service has everything we want to watch.
It's terrible that all the TV streaming services I now have cost me more than what I was paying for cable.
It's terrible that I can't completely cut the cord, because I need Internet to stream all my TV.
It's terrible when I'm too tired to do absolutely anything… except binge one more episode.
It's terrible that the reason why I'm tired is because I binged practically the whole season the night before.

It's terrible when I have to wait a week for my show's next episode.

It's terrible when I have to wait a year for my show's next season.

It's terrible that I still clap when the ***Friends*** theme song comes on TV.

It's terrible that anytime day or night you can find ***The Golden Girls*** on TV.

It's terrible that I've grown to love some TV shows because they play nonstop.

It's terrible that when I find time to watch a TV show, I always seem to catch the same damn episode.

Final Season

It's terrible that I'm SO behind on all my shows.
It's terrible that some great TV series are good to watch only once.
It's terrible when a show jumps the shark.
It's terrible when I need to find a new TV series to watch, to replace one that just ended.

It's terrible when a season finale is terrible.

Regardless of how it ended, it's tough when the TV shows we're addicted to come to an end. List your favorite canceled shows on the following TV menu. →

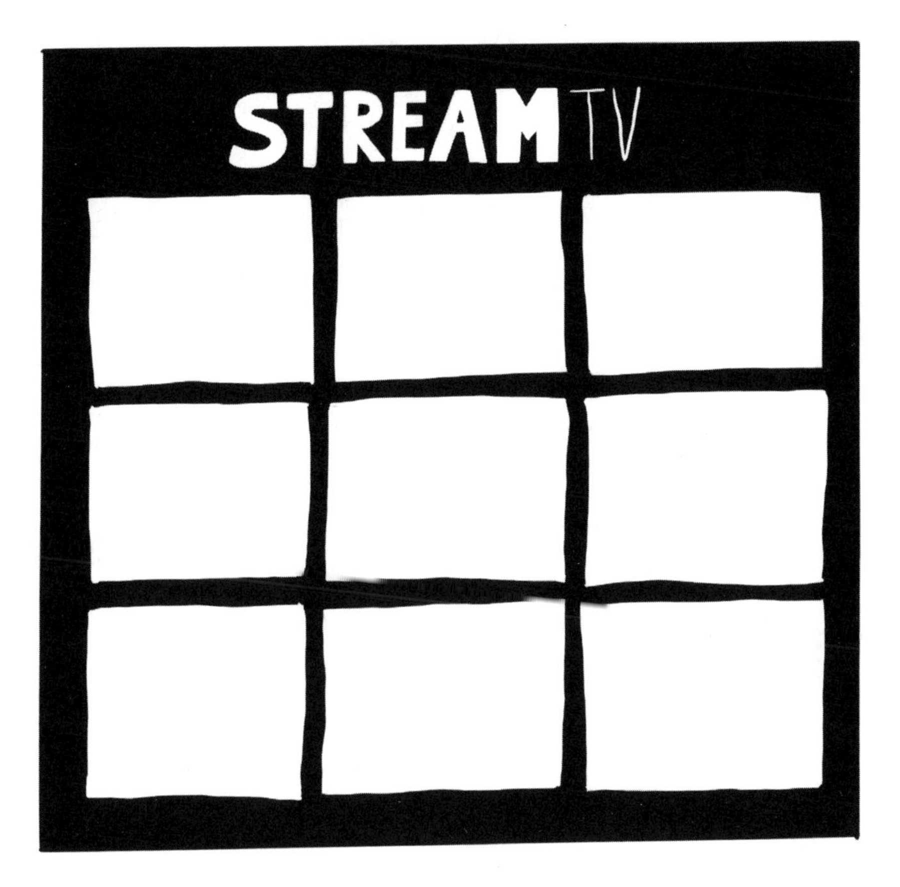

It’s terrible that the only things I read are
TV and takeout menus.

Out of Control

It's terrible when you need seven remote controls to watch TV.

It's terrible when you can't find the one remote control you need.

It's terrible that you don't know what one of those remotes controls.

It's terrible that we can't control people.

It's terrible that we let people control us.

We all have aspects of our lives that are out of control. On the dysfunctional remote, label the buttons with the things that you can't stop or change in your life. →

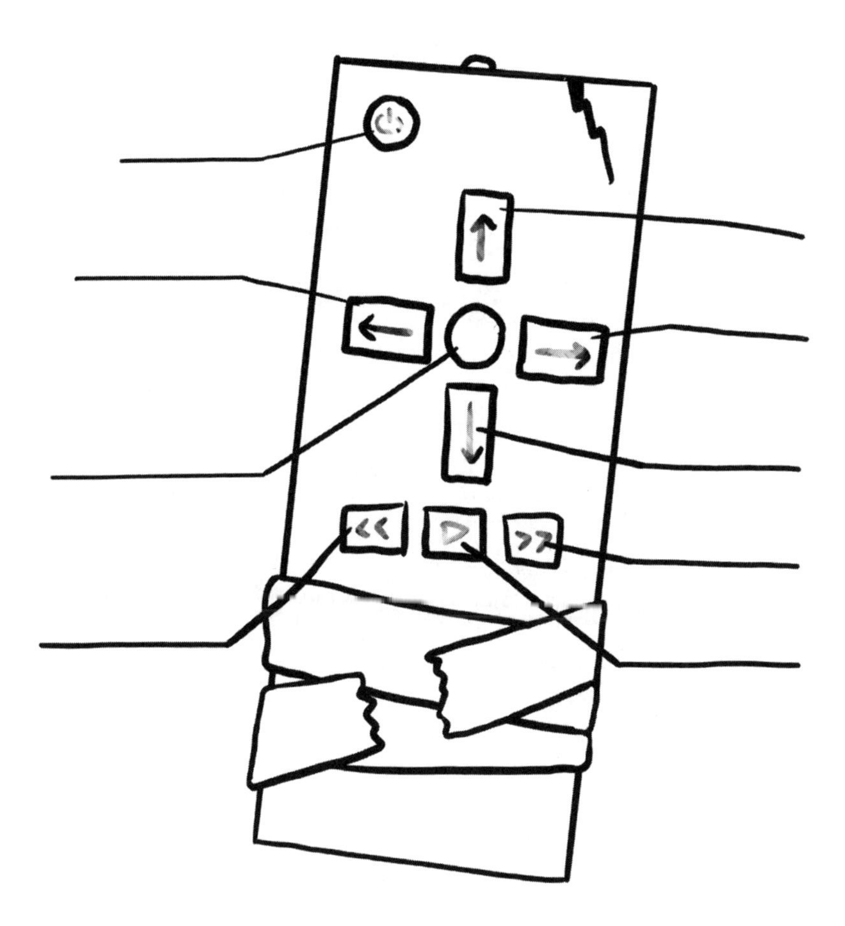

It’s terrible when you are out of control.

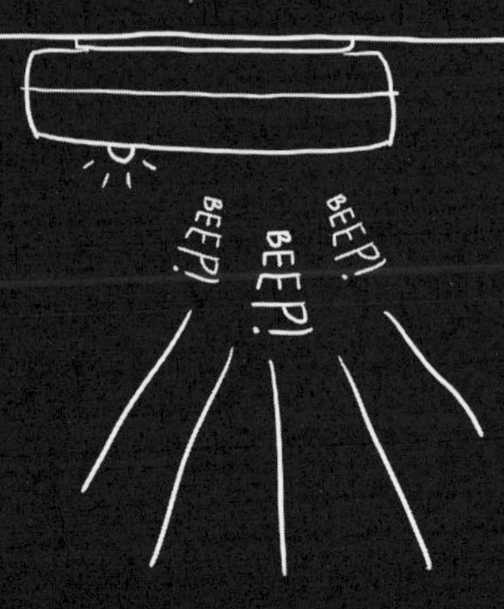

It's terrible how desperate you get when the batteries die
on the remote control.
It's terrible when you have to steal batteries from
something else just to change the damn channel.
It's terrible that there were times, not too long ago…when
you had to get up to change the channel manually.
It's terrible that the smoke alarm batteries always die
in the middle of the night.
It's terrible when you can't tell which smoke alarm's
batteries have died.
It's terrible that we ignore when someone's car alarm is
going off.
It's terrible when we ignore all the warnings signs.

It’s terrible when people whistle.

It’s terrible that people don’t just break out into song and dance like they do in 50s musicals.

It’s terrible that I’ll never walk a red carpet.

It’s terrible that nobody will ever ask me what I’m wearing.

It’s terrible when you can’t match your underwear to your attire.

It’s terrible when you want to set your entire wardrobe on fire and start again.

It's terrible that I have a closet and dresser full of clothes that I haven't worn in years.

It's terrible that I can't fit into half of the clothes I have.

It's terrible that I'll never fit into half of the clothes I have, ever again.

It's terrible that it's easier to buy new clothes than to lose weight to fit in the ones I have.

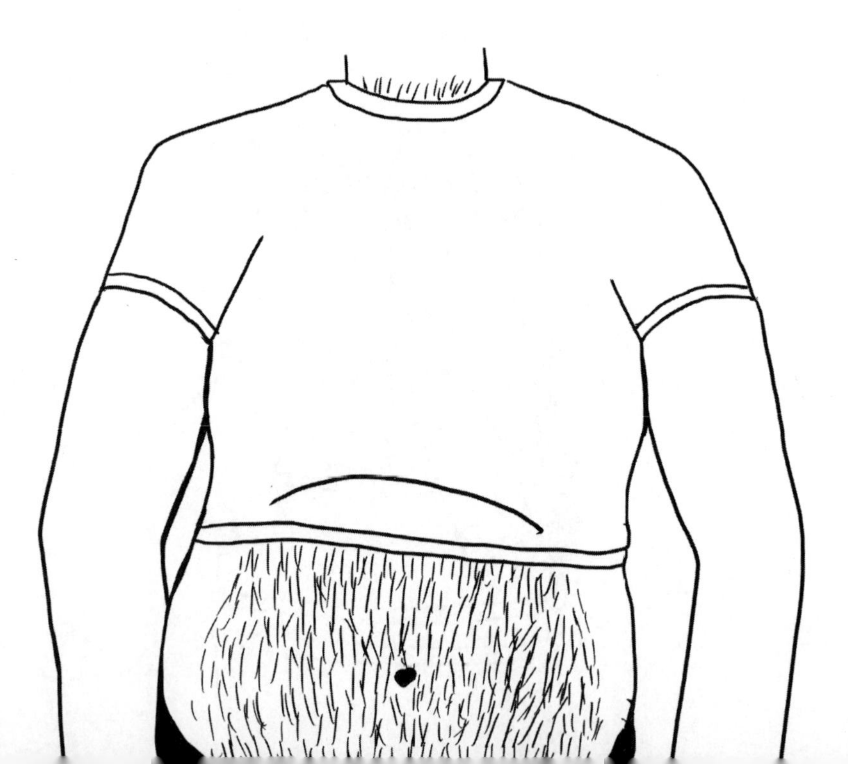

It's terrible when you keep clothes in the hope that they come back in style.
It's terrible when you had clothes so long that they have come back in style.
It's terrible when you can't keep up with the latest style.
It's terrible when you never like the latest style.
It's terrible when you have no style.

It's terrible when couples start sharing clothes.
It's terrible when people begin to resemble their pet.
It's terrible when your significant other doesn't like the same food as you.
It's terrible that it's my fault my pet loves all the same food as me.
It's terrible when people eat off my plate.
It's terrible that I let my pet lick my plate clean.
It's terrible that I brush my pet more than I groom myself.
It's terrible when your pet looks at you like you're crazy.

It's terrible that I believe I may be the only sane one left on this planet.

It's terrible that others actually think they are the only sane ones left too.

It's terrible when someone's crazy laugh is funnier than the joke.

It's terrible when the person you are with has an annoying laugh.

It's terrible when you laugh at something you shouldn't.

It's terrible when everything is so bad you just have to laugh.

It’s terrible that politics have become a joke.
It’s terrible when you are the butt of a joke.
It’s terrible that nobody inappropriately touches my butt.
It’s terrible how much I love affection.

Most of us have those spots that turn us on, but some of us also have places that we don't like touched. Write down what your off-limit spot is and why:

____

____

It’s terrible that if I want affection, I have to touch myself.

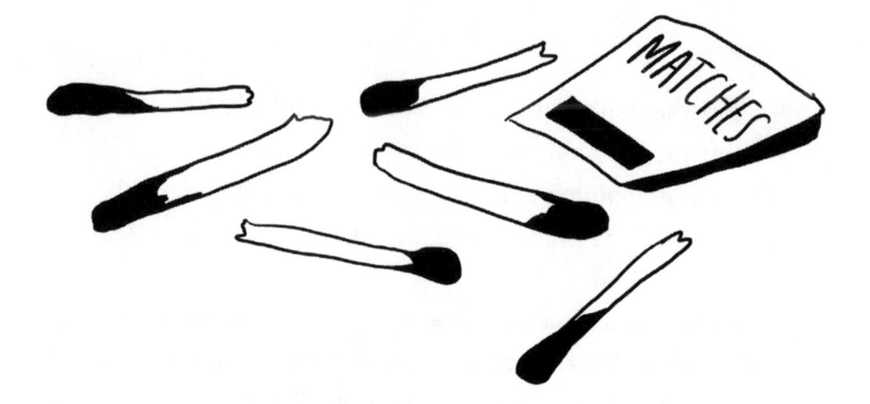

It’s terrible when the spark has gone out.
It’s terrible when you hope they get burned.
It’s terrible when the matches keep going out.
It’s terrible when you only have one left.
It’s terrible when it doesn’t come easy.
It’s terrible that it feels better when you have to work for it.

It's terrible when you have to commit to something.
It's terrible when you're not that interested.
It's terrible when there is a new shiny toy that catches your eye.
It's terrible when you forget that the toy you already have is perfectly fine.
It's terrible when you don't want your toy…until someone else wants it.
It's terrible when you aren't as shiny as you used to be.

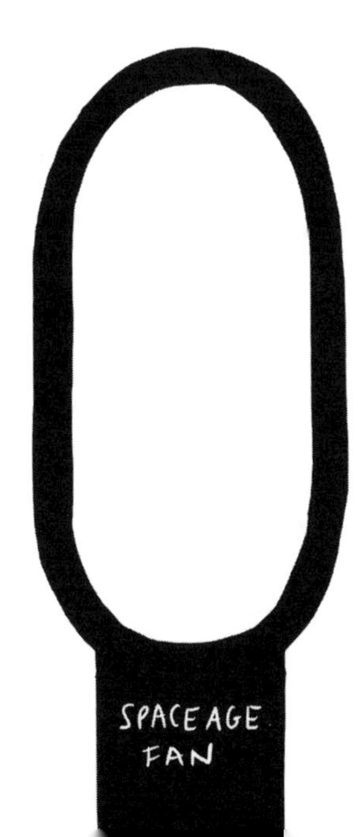

It's terrible that there are few things that can make everything better like a pet can.

It's terrible that nobody else's pet is as amazing as mine.

It's terrible that I tell my pet everything.

It's terrible that my pet is my best friend.

It's terrible that my pet is the only one who truly understands me.

It's terrible that I may love my pet more than I may ever love anyone.

It's terrible that I need my pet more than it needs me.

It’s terrible that I let my pet take the best seat in the house.

It’s terrible that I will go through great lengths to not disturb my pet while it’s sleeping.

It’s terrible that my little precious fur ball kicks me all night long.

It’s terrible that vets know you would pay anything to keep your pet healthy.

It’s terrible that they don’t yet allow cloning to keep your little fuzzy muffin-lovekin forever and ever and ever.

It’s terrible when I see people who are obsessed with their pets.

Terrible Pets

It's terrible that pets' names are cooler than people names.
It's terrible when kids name their pets.
It's terrible when kids aren't on a leash.
It's terrible when you have to wear a collared shirt.
It's terrible if no one has ever given you a pet name.
It's terrible when people think they can raise a perfectly behaved pet.
It's terrible that people are far from perfect, so why would their pets be any different?
It's terrible that people give their pets cute, cheery names that often don't suit their REAL personalities.

If you were to name pets according to their real-life traits, what names would you put on their name tags for all to see?

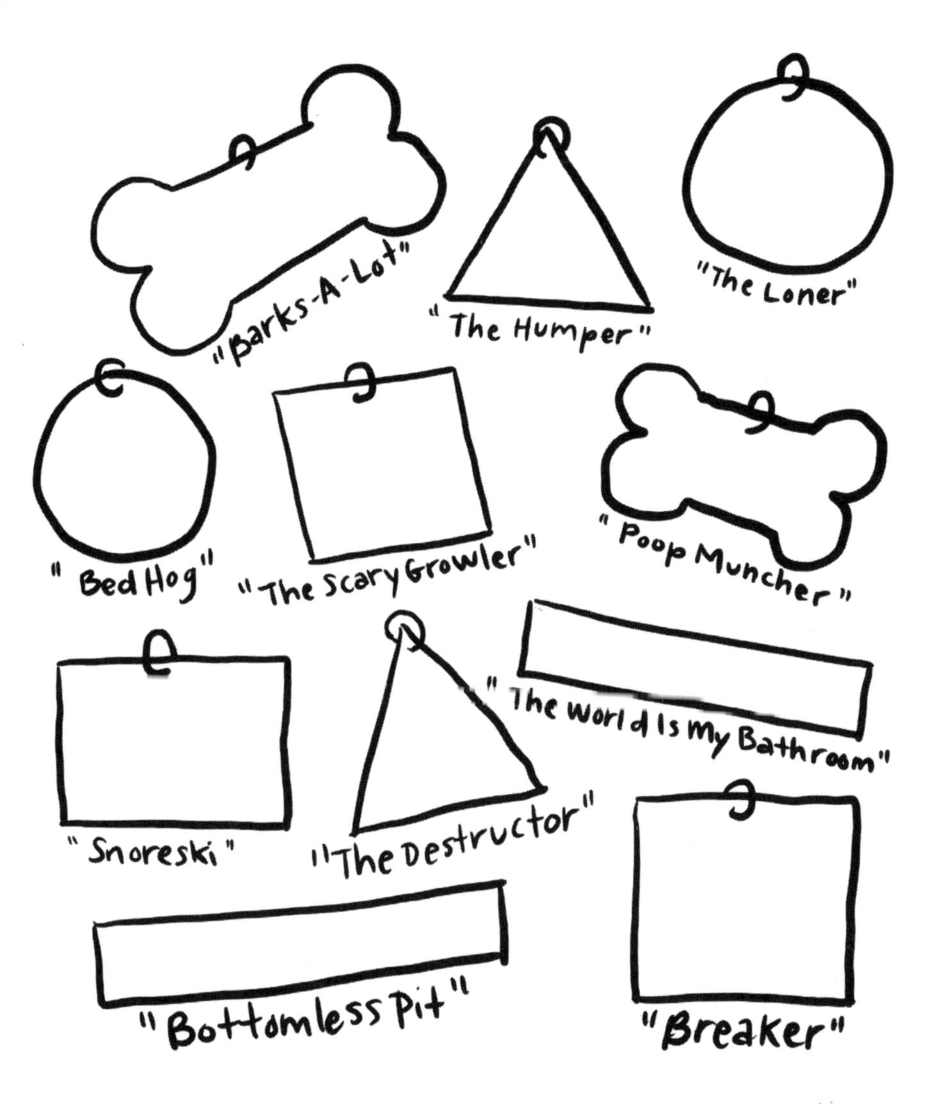

It's terrible that some people can't be neutered or spayed.

It's terrible that we can't train all pets to use the toilet.
It's terrible when the automatic toilet flushes while you're still on the toilet.
It's terrible when automatic soap dispensers dispense soap after you pull your hand away.
It's terrible when automatic faucets work for only 2 seconds.
It's terrible when you have to touch the automatic dispenser to get your paper towel.
It's terrible when you're done showering and forget to leave out a towel.

It's terrible when you forget to replace the soap…and have to wash your body with a tiny little soap nubbin.

It's terrible that you don't want to waste that tiny little soap nubbin.

It's terrible that soap, which is meant to clean, leaves scum behind that you have to clean.

It's terrible that I physically gag when I pull my own massive wad of stanky hair out of the clogged drain.

It's terrible when you have to pull someone else's stanky hair clog out of the drain.

A Hairy Situation

It's terrible when people are oblivious about their long protruding nose hair.

It's terrible when your new hairdresser has a bad hairdo.

It's terrible when the person you are with has nicer hair than you.

It's terrible when people compliment your hair, but you didn't even wash or do anything with it.

It's terrible how much hair I leave behind in the shower every day!

It's terrible how a bad hair day can affect the whole day.

Over the years, some pretty bad hairstyles and clothing fads have come and gone...and it's terrible that you may have gotten caught up in them.

Above the anatomy of the mullet, list all the worst hair and clothing trends you can think of.

Below "The Party" portion of the mullet, list all the fads and hairstyles that you now regret wearing out in public.

It's terrible when you catch on to a trend too late.

It's terrible to think of a time before shaving was a thing.

It's terrible if you were that kid in school who grew a beard long before everyone else.

It's terrible when teens attempt to grow a mustache.

If time machines were a thing, what do you think would be the worst time period to go back to? Write your answer on the following line:

____

It's terrible that time machines don't exist.

It's terrible when we just exist.

It's terrible that anyone would waste their time with going back to the past.
It's terrible that everything has been terrible long before us.
It's terrible that everything will be terrible long after us.
It's terrible that there is no way to know what the future holds.
It's terrible that we keep wanting things to come, versus enjoying the now.
It's terrible that we seldom get what we want.

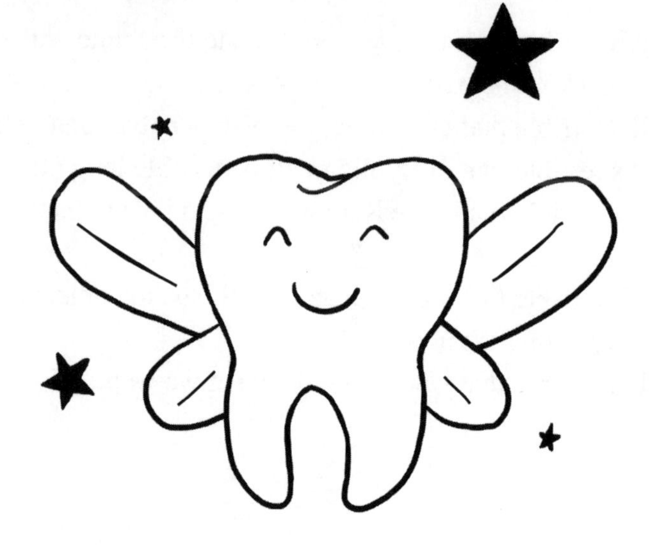

It's terrible when some people get everything they want.
It's terrible when nobody spoils you.
It's terrible if you don't spoil yourself.
It's terrible when you spoil your dinner.
It's terrible that I'm always hungry.
It's terrible that I look for something to eat, after
  I've just eaten.
It's terrible how much more the tooth fairy gives now
  than when I was a kid.

It's terrible that I have more pictures of the food that I ate last week than pictures of me when I was a kid.

It's terrible that kids have more advanced personal electronics than I do.

It's terrible when kids play with personal electronics at full volume.

It's terrible when kids are at full volume.

It's terrible when parents have nothing to talk about but their kids.

It's terrible that people don't have a volume control.

It's terrible getting invited to kids' birthday parties…when you don't have kids.

It's terrible when they don't have alcohol for the adults at kids' parties.

It's terrible when you keep losing your drink at the party.

It's terrible that everyone thinks their baby is the smartest baby ever.

It's terrible that I've never met a smart baby.

It's terrible that all parents think they are baby experts and share their advice whether you want it or not.

It's terrible that I've learned what not to do as a parent by watching other parents.

YOU'RE INVITED

TO

Bobby's 2nd Birthday

THIS SATURDAY

at 1:00 pm

Please bring a $50 gift!

Snacks will be served.

BYOB

It's terrible that the children are our future.

It's terrible that we can't go back and do it again.

Bad Names

It's terrible when a baby doesn't look like their name.
It's terrible that I don't find other people's babies cute.
It's terrible that I don't like the smell of babies.
It's terrible that just when a kid is getting a personality, that's when they are most terrible.
It's terrible that no one names their babies awesome historic names like Ivan the Terrible, Thor, Madonna, or Cher.

Throughout your life, you've probably met some pretty terrible people, and, as a result, their names probably leave a bad taste in your mouth. Because of those people, what are the names that you would NEVER consider giving a child of your own someday?

It's terrible that no matter how long it's been, we just can't let some things go.

It's terrible that I'm more immature than most kids.

Getting Hangry

It's terrible when there is nothing in the fridge to eat, no matter how many times you look.
It's terrible when you aren't allowed to leave the table until you've finished your food.
It's terrible when you can't get up from the table because you've finished ALL the food.

Growing up, we all had those foods that we absolutely hated but had to eat anyway. On this menu, list the foods that you wouldn't eat now if your life depended on it.

My LEAST Favorite Foods Menu

DRINKS

SNACKS

MAIN DISHES

VEGGIES/FRUITS

DESSERTS

And, My Least Favorite Regional Food Is:

It's terrible that my computer runs updates four times a day.
It's terrible that my body doesn't run until I've had coffee.
It's terrible that I need ongoing coffee intake to keep my burners going all day.
It's terrible when the coffee has been on the burner too long.
It's terrible how much I spend on coffee.
It's terrible when you need coffee to do your daily duty.
It's terrible how anal-retentive I am.

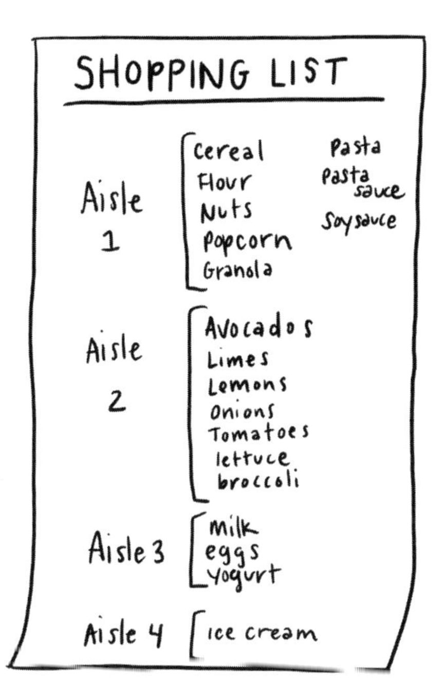

It's terrible that I need to write my shopping list in the order the items are found at the grocery store.
It's terrible when they rearrange the grocery store.
It's terrible that I fear change.
It's terrible that my biggest fear is that nothing will change.
It's terrible that we forget that one person CAN make a change.
It's terrible that I'm not that person.

We're Doomed

It's terrible that we live in such a disposable society.
It's terrible when we think it's just one bottle of water, what could that hurt?
It's terrible when the world's population thinks that way too....
It's terrible that ignorance is easy.
It's terrible that making change is hard.
It's terrible when one thing affects another.
It's terrible that once it's gone, it's gone.

Let's face it: The outlook isn't good. We've been focusing in this book on the things around us, but the whole world is a mess.

What are those BIG terrible things that people don't like to talk about but should? Write one in each box.

It’s terrible that we all have bigger problems.

It's terrible when it's you against the world.
It's terrible that some people don't have a care in the world.
It's terrible that I care more for everyone else than myself.
It's terrible that all my dog cares about is sleeping, eating, and humping.
It's terrible when you realize that your priorities are all wrong.

It’s terrible that my diet always starts tomorrow.
It’s terrible when you start your diet and realize how many pounds you have to lose.
It’s terrible when you count down the minutes until lunchtime.
It’s terrible that my fitness band reminds me how unfit I am.
It’s terrible that when I see my blood pressure on my fitness band, it makes it go up further.
It’s terrible that I lie there all night thinking about how my fitness band is going to tell me that I didn’t get a good night’s sleep.
It’s terrible that workout clothes are more comfortable for loafing out in.

It's terrible that there is even something called a marathon.
It's terrible that my heart races just seeing someone who is out of my league.
It's terrible that I can't even finish lacing my shoes without getting winded.
It's terrible that I'm thinking of switching to Velcro.

It's terrible that, with all the food references, you must think I weigh 900 pounds.

It's terrible that we have a nervous laugh when in an uncomfortable situation.

It's terrible that we have to follow a joke with a haha, jk, or LOL so they know we are joking. Hehe.

It's terrible when they don't take anything seriously.

It's terrible how easily a harmless text message can be misconstrued.

It's terrible that autocorrect would butcher the word "misconstrued."

It's turribile that I doesn't proofreed my text befores I sended it.

It's terrible when they don't send a reply.

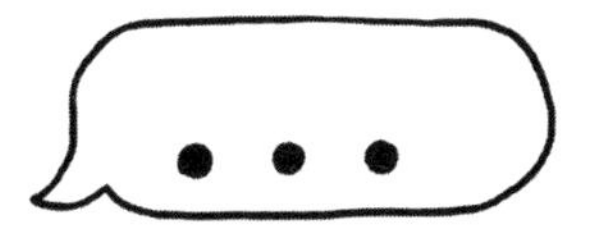

It's terrible that wherever you look, someone is staring into their phone.

It's terrible when someone is paying more attention to their phone than you.

It's terrible that people text one another in place of having a real conversation.

It's terrible when someone calls in place of sending a text.

It's terrible how poorly AF grammar has gotten thanks to txt msgs. WTH! Smh

It's terrible when people overuse emojis and acronyms. Which emojis and acronyms drive you crazy the most? Write or draw them out.

It's terrible that I get more spam texts than messages from my friends.

It's terrible that whenever my phone rings, it's either an emergency or an annoying spam/robo call.

It's terrible that I've still yet to receive my free vacation, school loan payoff, or new job.

It's terrible that nobody wishes you a happy birthday via a phone call any longer.

It's terrible if there is more than one name on your birthday cake.

It's terrible when you have to work on your birthday.

It's terrible when people have holidays off, but you don't.

It's terrible when you forget to remove the price on a gift.

It's terrible when people intentionally leave the price on a gift.

It’s terrible when you are in a gift swap and you spent more on their gift.

It’s terrible when someone regifts a gift you gave, back to you.

It’s terrible when you are not good at faking that you like a gift.

It’s terrible when you get a reused gift bag with someone else’s name on it.

It’s terrible when you use a gift bag because you are too lazy to wrap.

It’s terrible when the tissue paper was reused too many times.

It's terrible when someone uses Christmas paper for a birthday gift.

It's terrible if you get a combined Christmas/birthday gift.

It's terrible when you cut your wrapping paper just a ***little*** too short.

It's terrible when you can't get the back off those cheap bows.

It's terrible when people go in on a gift together.

It's terrible when people don't realize your presence is gift enough.

It's terrible when the number of candles on your birthday cake become a fire hazard.

It's terrible when someone else blows out your birthday candles.

It's terrible when your birthday wish is the same as last year.

It's terrible that someone else has probably made a wish on your shooting star.

It's terrible when you go to toss a coin into a fountain and miss.

It's terrible that someone takes your "wish" coin from the fountain and spends it.

You've tried and tried, with no luck. What is that one wish that you keep wishing for that seems to never come true?

____

____

It's terrible when someone gets rich on an idea that you had.

YOU LOSE

It's terrible that we've all daydreamed about winning the lottery.

It's terrible that we'll likely never get to quit our job in a spectacular way.

It's terrible that somebody else actually does get to do that when they win.

It's terrible that I don't know anyone who has won the lottery.

It's terrible that I only play the lottery when it's over $100 million, because anything less isn't worth my time.

It's terrible that ***maybe*** my standards are too high.

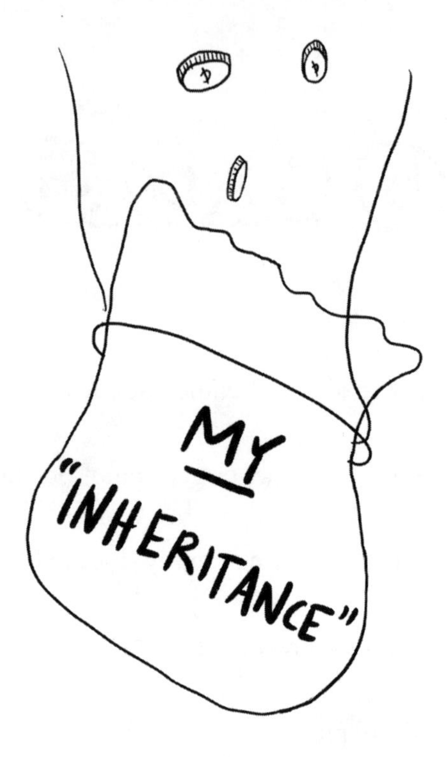

It's terrible when I see my parents spending my inheritance.

It's terrible that I want my parents to slow down and enjoy their golden years…just not too much.

It's terrible that women outlive men.

It's terrible when it's all a matter of perspective….

It's terrible that not everyone knows which way the toilet paper is supposed to hang.
It's terrible that everyone else is wrong.

Okay, this might be a deal breaker between us, but which way do you hang your toilet paper? Over or under?

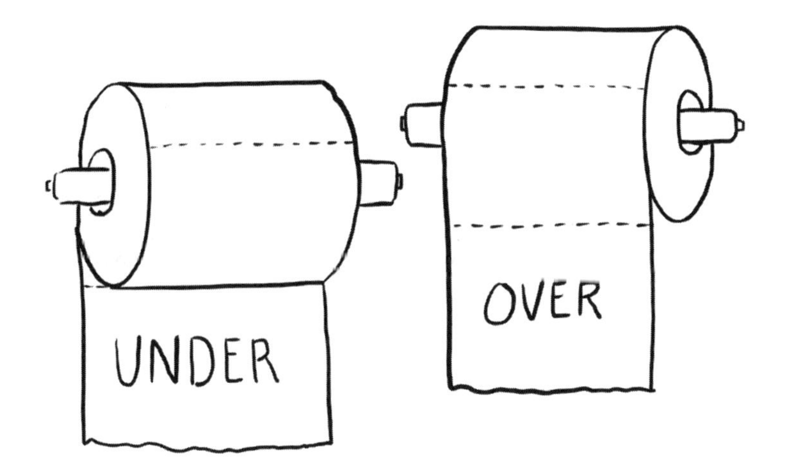

It's terrible if you didn't choose "over."

This is just a reminder that even though it may ***sometimes*** seem like there is hope, trust me…

…everything is still terrible.

Going Postal

It's terrible that the only mail I get goes right to the garbage.

It's terrible when they get your postcard two weeks after you've arrived home.

It's terrible when your home state turns up in the "worst states to live" lists.

It's terrible that each state has its own list of things that people love to complain about.

If you were to send postcards from your state that only highlight the terrible things about where you live, what would those postcards look like? Be sure to include your terrible state's name!

It's terrible when people give your state a bad reputation.

It's terrible when you are proud of your state's bad reputation.

Creepy-Crawly

It's terrible that bugs can lift one hundred times their own weight.

It's terrible that bugs can climb walls and fall from great heights and walk away just fine.

It's terrible that bugs have more legs and eyes than you.

It's terrible that there are way more bugs than humans.

It's terrible that bugs can find their way indoors.

It's terrible that you are usually defenseless when you have to face off against a bug with all those eyes and legs and super speed creeping toward you.

I'm sure your imagination is more vivid than mine, so draw your worst nightmare of a bug and define its strengths and weaknesses. Your shoe isn't likely going to help with this horrible creature!

→

It's terrible that 86% of the world's species are still unknown, so this bug...may just really exist.

BIG and Small

It's terrible when you have to break a spine of a perfectly healthy new book.
It's terrible that I judge a book by its cover.
It's terrible that most will judge this book by its cover.
It's terrible that there are enough terrible things to fill a book this size.
It's terrible that bigger isn't always better.

When I do things, I like to go BIG or go home. But bigger things aren't always better. And maybe even worse, small things can suck in big ways too. For instance, there are big things from Earth-ending asteroids to romance-ending, big-ugly granny panties to small things that are a pain in the ass, like angry little Chihuahuas to fiery little hemorrhoids.

With those examples in mind, what are the BIGGEST and smallest things that you can think of that suck BIG-time?

THIS LIST IS FOR THE BIG TERRIBLE THINGS

This list is for all the small things that really suck in BIG ways

It's terrible when going too big was a bad idea.

It's terrible that they've made it so you should upgrade
EVERY light bulb in your home.
It's terrible when you need to upgrade everything in your
home.
It's terrible that it's not as easy to upgrade everything in
your life.
It's terrible that the new light bulbs are supposed to last for
ten years…but last one-tenth of that time.
It's terrible that the new light bulbs cost ten times
the old ones.
It's terrible that I have ten different shades
of white light bulbs.

It’s terrible when people keep you in the dark.
It’s terrible when you are always the last to know.
It’s terrible when you are better off not knowing.
It’s terrible when people are know-it-alls.
It’s terrible that they really don’t know the half of it all.

It's terrible when you get into someone's car and it's blasting talk radio.

It's terrible when there is that one annoying radio show sidekick who makes you want to turn off the radio.

It's terrible when your GPS speaks directions over your favorite song.

It's terrible that you likely have heard that there is this small-town girl, who lives in a lonely world, and she takes a midnight train to anywhere....

It's terrible that we sing about this stranger's depressing life at the top of our lungs whenever it comes on.

It's terrible when you "stop believin'."

It's terrible that I just heard there was a city boy, born in South Detroit, but I'm less interested in him.

It's terrible when a good song makes you drive faster.

We all have them, so write down the name of that song that makes you drive faster and likely will get you pulled over for speeding.

____

____

It's terrible when you've been driving under the speed limit for 38 miles, because you thought it was a police car behind you.

It's terrible that concert tickets cost SO much.

It's terrible that there are so many music artists I'll never get to see.

It's terrible when you finally do make it to a concert and can only see the artist on the big screen.

It's terrible that parking costs almost as much as the concert tickets.

It's terrible that if you want to save a few bucks, you have to buy a terrible knockoff shirt in the parking lot from some hairy guy…not wearing a shirt.

It’s terrible if you’re not doing what you dreamed you’d be doing when you grew up.
It’s terrible that I still don’t know what I want to do when I grow up.
It’s terrible that I don’t feel like a grownup.
It’s terrible that I have the responsibilities of a grownup.
It’s terrible that OTHER people have figured out how to make money playing video games.
It’s terrible that I haven’t figured out anything yet. . . .

It’s terrible that people fall for pyramid schemes.
It’s terrible when they try to pull you into their pyramid scheme.
It’s terrible that most of us will never get to see the pyramids.
It’s terrible when you eat something that has gotten sand in it.
It’s terrible when you see yet another person’s photo bragging that they are at the beach.
It’s terrible that I can’t quit social media, because I don’t want to miss anything.
It’s terrible that because I stare into my phone all day, I do miss everything.

It's terrible when you try to call customer service…and it's automated.

It's terrible that automated customer service brings 0 value to anyone.

It's terrible that I don't complain enough.

It's terrible that it's stereotypical for me to just deal with the crap.

Not that anything would get done about it, but what's one thing that you don't complain about but should?

____

____

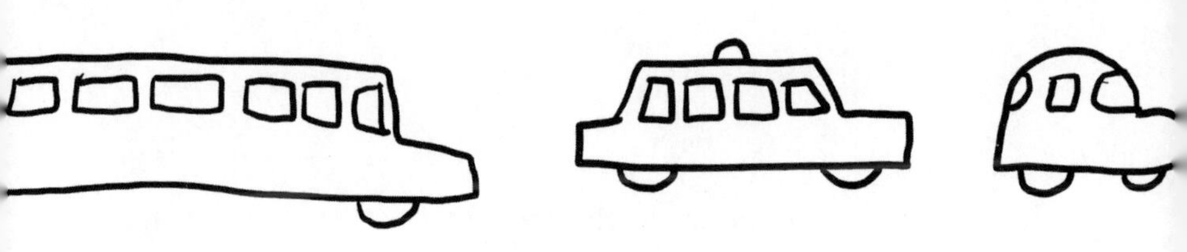

It's terrible when you have to speed to keep up with traffic.

It's terrible when you're speeding down the highway and have to come to a complete stop.

It's terrible when the car behind you didn't stop.

It's terrible that there is no such thing as a happy little accident.

It's terrible when the person behind you honks because you didn't move up the 2 inches you have to spare.

It's terrible when the traffic is always going in the same direction as you.

It's terrible when you can't go with the flow.

It's terrible when they pass you, then slow down.

It's terrible how annoyed I get when someone doesn't let me into traffic.

It's terrible that I don't let others into traffic.

It's terrible that I honk at student drivers for going too slow.

Vanity

It's terrible when people talk to their pets or kids using
a baby voice.
It's terrible that I often mutter to myself.
It's terrible that I talk to my car.
It's terrible it listens better than most.

Some of the worst people you encounter are on the roads with you. Use the front vanity plate on the next page to write a message to all the terrible people who see you and your car coming in their rearview mirror. Then use the back vanity plate to write a message for those terrible people to see when you pass them.

MY FRONT PLATE

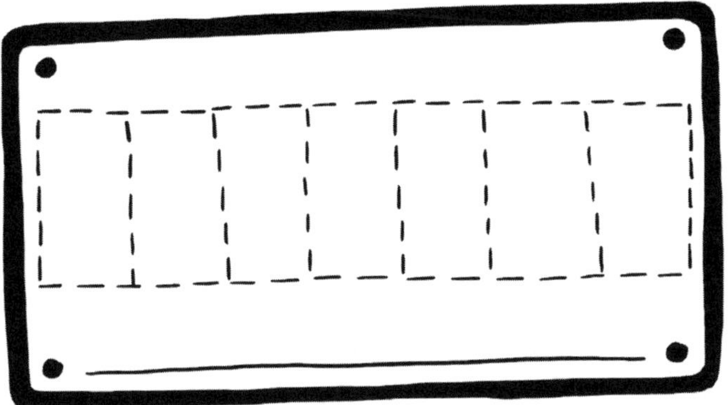

MY BACK PLATE

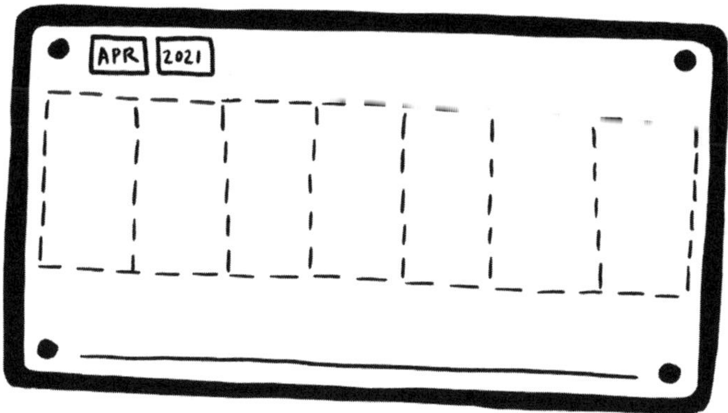

It’s terrible when there are limits.

It’s terrible when there are no limits.

It’s terrible when you don’t know your limits.

It's terrible when kids in cars wave at you while you are driving…and you are already busy doing three other things.

It's terrible when you're not a good multitasker.

It's terrible when the car doing 80 in front of you washes their windshield…and yours too.

It's terrible when your auto-sensing windshield wipers have an annoying mind of their own.

It's terrible when people let their windshield wipers screech across a dry window.

It's terrible when people drive you nuts.

It's terrible that cars depreciate so much when you drive
them off the lot.
It's terrible when you can barely get your old clunker home
from your work's lot.
It's terrible when your car breaks down more than you do.

It's terrible that I've been told I'm an aggressive driver.
It's terrible when you have to tailgate so someone doesn't cut in front of you.
It's terrible when people would rather drive in place of you driving.
It's terrible when people take better care of their car than they do themselves.

It's terrible when you get a chip in your car windshield.
It's terrible when your favorite mug gets a chip in it.
It's terrible when you walk around with a chip on your shoulder.
It's terrible when someone doesn't close up the bag of chips.
It's terrible that we let so much food expire.
It's terrible when you perspire from running to catch the parking meter before it expires.
It's terrible when you run into a pothole and get a flat tire.
It's terrible how much I love doughnuts.

It's terrible when things fly out of the dump truck that you are behind.
It's terrible when you realize that your pants make your behind look dumpy.
It's terrible that it's so hard to find pants to make your behind look good.
It's terrible that I've never tried to look or dress badass.
It's terrible that I don't try too hard on much of anything.
It's terrible how hard I can be on myself.
It's terrible that nothing on my body is hard.

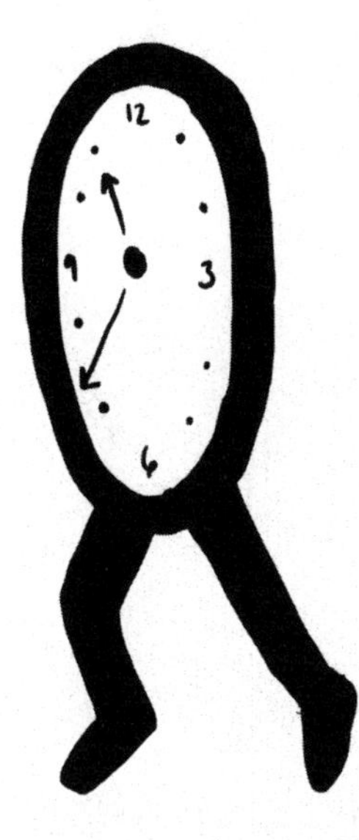

It's terrible if you hit puberty well behind everyone else.

It's terrible when you are so far behind and feel you will never catch up.

It's terrible that we can't take our time.

It's terrible that we are running out of time.

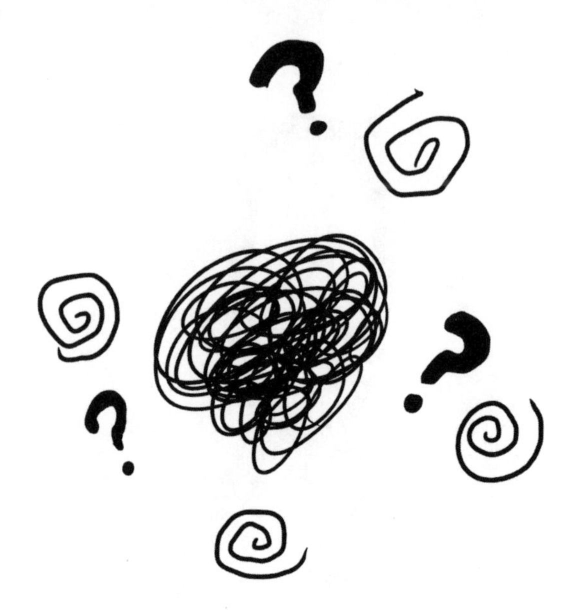

It's terrible when you are easily confused.
It's terrible when something is missing.
It's terrible when someone moves your cheese.
It's terrible when someone doesn't put it back where it belongs.
It's terrible when you don't see eye to eye.
It's terrible when you're lost.

It's terrible that my GPS is not up to date.
It's terrible when you haven't been on a date in a while, and you find your GPS's voice sexy.
It's terrible that I argue with my GPS.
It's terrible when the GPS wins the argument.
It's terrible that I never win anything.
It's terrible that today, everyone gets a trophy.
It's terrible that Ricky Bobby taught me, "If you ain't first, you're last."
It's terrible that my most inspiring quotes are from comedy movies.

It's terrible that "wherever you go, there you are."
But it's more terrible if "you shall not pass."

It's terrible if you are told to "live long and prosper."
But it's more terrible if you're unable to "make it so."

It's terrible if you "are not in Kansas anymore."
But it's more terrible if you're where "the sh*t is hitting the fan."

It's terrible when you learn you've been misquoting a movie line wrong for years.
It's even more terrible if you ever gave 110%, raised the bar, thought outside the box, or actually used a "business catchphrase" in or out of the workplace.

It's terrible when you are put in a box.
It's terrible when you are unable to think outside the box.
It's terrible when you are comfortable in your safe little box.
It's terrible when they want a little blue Tiffany box.
It's terrible that when you open some boxes, what comes out can't be put back.

It's terrible when you are pressured to put a ring on it.
It's terrible that only fantasy lovers know there is one ring to rule them all.
It's terrible when you shoulda put a ring on it.
It's terrible when getting a ring doesn't live up to the fantasy you've always dreamed of.
It's terrible when you have to get into a ring to fight for what you want.

It’s terrible when you’d rather watch ***Netflix*** than chill.

It’s terrible when you get cold feet.

It’s terrible when you don’t understand why you are getting the cold shoulder.

It’s terrible that regardless of how warm it is outside, some people are always cold.

Most people identify as either a frozen popsicle or as a human heater. Either way, being one of these extremes is terrible for you and for whoever you may wish to cuddle with at night. Circle the one you are:

Frozen Popsicle   Human Heater

It’s terrible when your partner is too much like you.

It’s terrible when it snows on a weekend and you don’t get a snow day.
It’s terrible when it’s the dead of winter and your skin is all dry and itchy.
It’s terrible when allergy season starts.
It’s terrible when it’s all hot and sticky out.
It’s terrible when you have to rake up your neighbor’s leaves in your yard.

It's terrible when it's the same thing every year.

Everyone has a season that they love, but which do you dislike the most and why?
Number them in order 1–4, with 4 being the worst.

1. ____________ **3.** ____________

2. ____________ **4.** ____________

What is it about the worst season that is so terrible?

____

It's terrible that though the summer just started, the days
start getting shorter.
It's terrible that whenever we adjust for daylight saving
time in either direction, I seem to lose an hour of sleep.
It's terrible that nothing ever springs forward.
It's terrible that everything seems to fall back.

It's terrible that there are so few holidays off between January and May.

It's terrible that Valentine's Day is in a cold month…and colder if you are alone.

It's terrible that March brings winds and April brings showers so that May can bring allergies.

It's terrible that before you know it, the year is half over.

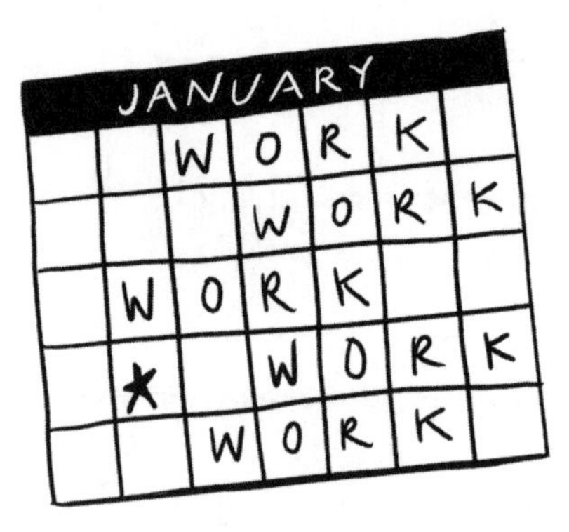

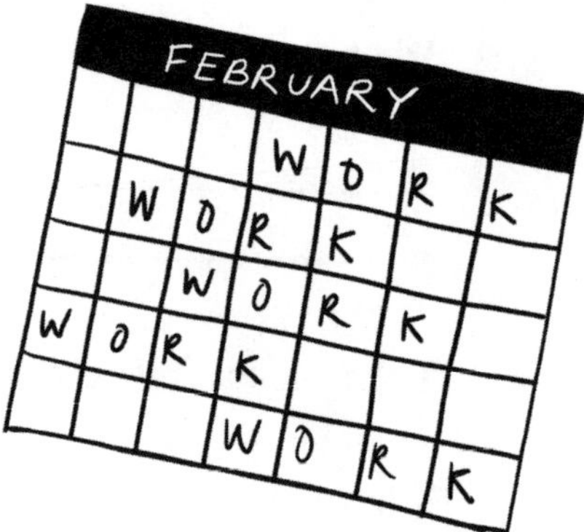

You've identified your least favorite season. Now write down which month you dislike the most and what it is about this month that is so terrible.

____

____

It's terrible when you have to share your birth month.

It's terrible that Sundays are no longer considered a day of rest.

It's terrible that we can fill a book about why Mondays are terrible.

It's terrible when it's not Taco Tuesday.

It's terrible that Wednesday has a hump.

It's terrible that more days don't have hope like Thursday.

It's terrible that Friday is my second favorite f-word.

It's terrible when you have chores, homework, or work on a Saturday.

It's terrible when you start dreading Monday on Sunday.

It's terrible that weekend hours go at least two times faster than weekday hours.

It's terrible when, at work on Thursday, you realize it's only Tuesday.

It's terrible when it's Wednesday and you have to wait another week for tacos.

It's pretty universal which days of the week are the best and worst, but feel free to correct if needed. And if Monday isn't the worst day for you, which is and why?

____

____

It's terrible that we all complain about the same things.

It's terrible that nobody does anything about it.

It's terrible that we all just assume someone else will take care of it.

It’s terrible when you have the same New Year’s resolution every year.

It’s terrible that we only get an extra day every four years.

It’s terrible that the years just keep flying by.

It’s terrible that when a new year starts, we actually believe it’ll be a better year.

It’s terrible when you know going into it that it’s going to be a bad year.

Everyone has at least one year that stands out as the worst year of their life. No need to recap why, but what was that terrible year that you'd like to erase or redo if you could? Fill in that year on the time stamp.

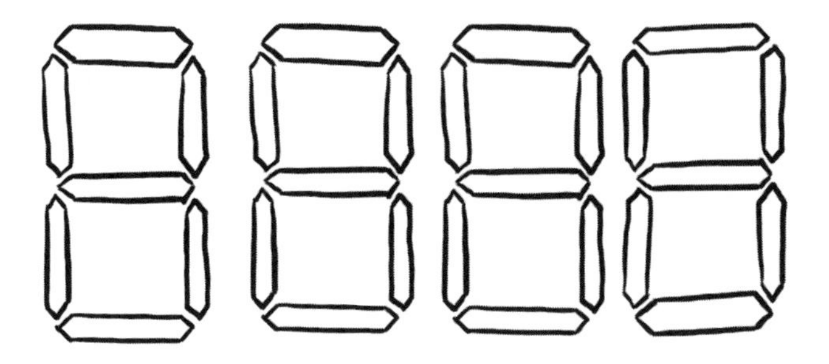

It's terrible when people bring up bad memories.

It's terrible when bad memories override the good memories.

It's terrible that we forget we can make new good memories every day.

It's terrible when people try to cheer you up.

It’s terrible that they serve pumpkin spice before summer is over.

It’s terrible that stores have Christmas decorations for sale the day before Halloween.

It’s terrible that everything is a little creepier in October.

It’s terrible that, as a kid, you’ll walk a mile to go to the house that gives out full-size candy bars on Halloween.

It’s terrible when you’re an adult and the house next to you gives out the full-size candy bars.

It’s terrible how your perspective changes when you get older.

It's terrible when you get too old to trick-or-treat.
It's terrible when the big kids come to your door for candy.
It's terrible when they don't even try to wear a costume.
It's terrible when someone has to ask what you are dressed as on Halloween.
It's terrible that we sometimes wish we were someone else.

I Got a Rock

It's terrible when your parents raid your trick-or-treat goody haul.
It's terrible when people run out of candy on Halloween and use their kid's candy as a backup.
It's terrible when you turn out the lights and try to be quiet to avoid the trick-or-treaters.
It's terrible when there are more tricks than treats.

We put a lot of effort into our Halloween costumes, but some homes are just terrible at knowing what we'd like to get in our Halloween haul. Rate each of the trick-or-treat goody bag items by filling in the ratings circles using the following rating system:

●○○○○ **1. Not too bad**
●●○○○ **2. Seriously?!**
●●●○○ **3. Why bother?**
●●●●○ **4. Going right into the garbage**
●●●●● **5. This house will get egged next mischief night**

It's terrible that people put out a bowl of candy and believe trick-or-treaters will take just one.

It's terrible that you can't wear white after Labor Day.
It's terrible when it doesn't snow on Christmas.
It's terrible that they start selling holiday decorations
before I've even taken mine down from last year.

It's terrible when Cupid doesn't do his job on Valentine's Day.

It's terrible that everybody is Irish on St. Patrick's Day.

It's terrible that it's also called the Fourth of July in other countries.

It's terrible that from Thanksgiving through January 1, I can count on wearing my fat pants.

It's terrible when your fat pants no longer fit.

We only get a few holidays each year, and as with everything, there is always something we can complain about. What is the worst holiday to celebrate?

____

____

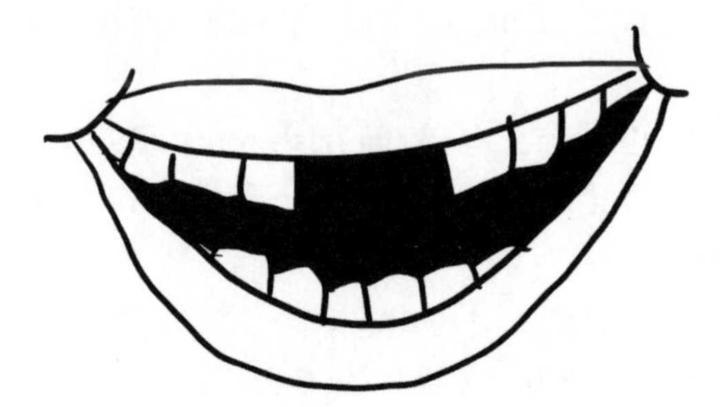

It's terrible if all you want for Christmas are your two front teeth.

It's terrible that all I want for Christmas is for Mariah Carey to have a different Christmas song for every station to play four hundred times a day.

It's terrible that though they played Christmas music for two months straight, they stop playing Christmas music on Christmas night.

It's terrible that come November 1, I'll be craving Christmas music again.

It's terrible that the Christmas spirit doesn't last for more than one day a year.

While Santa keeps a naughty list, we'd like you to list the 3 worst Christmas songs of all time.

Bad: ____________________

Worse: ____________________

Worst: ____________________

It's terrible that yule have to hear these songs again and again.

It's terrible when people use bad puns.

It’s terrible that we no longer believe in Santa.

It’s terrible if you still believed in Santa until now.

'Tis the Season

It's terrible that figgy pudding isn't pudding at all.

It's terrible that while the stretch of holidays at the end of the year can be such a joyous time...there is so much that can be terrible at the same time. If you were to write a new "Twelve Days of..." song (sung to the tune of "The Twelve Days of Christmas"), what are *12 TERRIBLE THINGS* about the holidays that would fill the song lines for you?

12 ______________________

11 ______________________

10 ______________________

9 ______________________

8 ______________________

It’s terrible that the Grinch’s heart will grow three sizes the day he reads this book.

It's terrible when what I want is off-limits.

It's terrible when someone opens something that is a limited edition.

It's terrible when you have to buy one to use and one to save.

What is that thing that you have and that you will never use because you want to keep it new in its package or you don't want to use it up?

____

It's terrible that we've barely tapped our unlimited potential.

It's terrible that what I have left to give is limited.

It's terrible that we have time limits…and the end is closer every minute.

It's terrible when terms aren't limited enough.

It's terrible that stupidity has no limits.

It's terrible when we reach our limits.

It’s terrible that the Force isn’t strong with me.
It’s terrible that when someone says, “May the Force be with you,” I reply, “And also with you.”
It’s terrible that he named the dog Indiana.
It’s terrible that the Terminator got old and won’t be back.
It’s terrible that I was never allowed to get a BB gun because Ralphie shot his eye out.
It’s terrible when they play holiday movies off-season.
It’s terrible that the holiday isn’t complete until Kevin McCallister gets left home alone…twice.
It’s terrible that there will never be another new John Hughes movie.
It’s terrible when the gosh darn Catalina Wine Mixer scene is played on G-rated TV.

It’s terrible when regular TV makes your favorite movie lines G-rated.

It’s terrible that I don’t know how my glasses get so dirty.
It’s terrible to think how dirty the rest of me might be.
It’s terrible that others don’t know how dirty I really am.
It’s terrible that other people are SO dirty.
It’s terrible that I don’t want to touch anything.
It’s terrible that money is so dirty.
It’s terrible that I don’t have money in my hands for long.

It's terrible that there is a bank on every corner, but I don't have any more money.

It's terrible that there is a pharmacy on every opposite corner…and now we know where the money is coming from.

It's terrible when you are sick of it all.

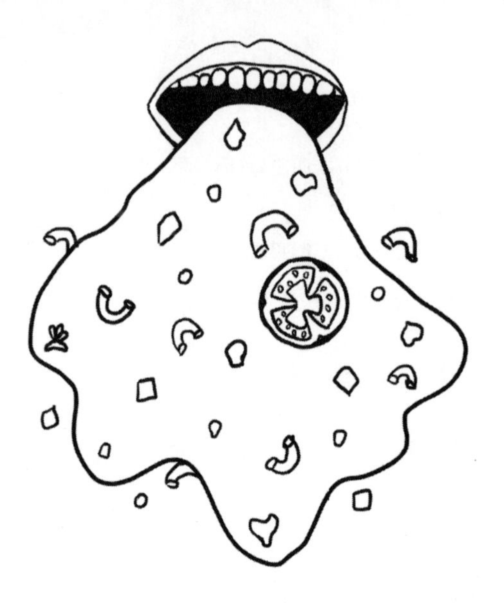

It’s terrible when people throwing up makes you want to throw up.

It’s terrible when you get sick on a weekend.

It’s terrible when you are more organized than your doctor’s office.

It’s terrible when you have to wait for your diagnosis.

It’s terrible when service people don’t call you back.

It’s terrible when you have to pay for something to be fixed again.

It’s terrible when something can’t be fixed.

It’s terrible when you’re pretty sure your warranty has expired.

It’s terrible when you feel like you no longer have it.
It’s terrible if someone took it from you.
It’s terrible when you’re wrong.
It’s terrible when you can’t tell right from wrong.
It’s terrible when there’s nothing left.
It’s terrible if it was never there in the first place.

EVERYTHING WILL BE TERRIBLE.

It's terrible when you've given up trying.
It's terrible when there is little left in this world that will still motivate you.
It's terrible when you're not counting on any motivation coming from anyone, anyway.
It's terrible that you CAN count on one thing… everything WILL BE terrible.

It's terrible when you wonder…how did everything get to
be so terrible?
It's terrible when you begin to question everything.
It's terrible when you get a nail in your tire.
It's terrible when you wonder…why are all these nails all
over our roads?
It's terrible when you wonder…how did ANOTHER shoe
get lost on the highway?
It's terrible when you experience déjà vu.

It's terrible when you experience déjà vu.

It's terrible how many new reusable bags I buy, because I keep forgetting mine.

It's terrible when there are twenty registers, but only two are open.

It's terrible when all of the self-checkout registers aren't turned on.

It's terrible when the lines are even longer in the speedy self-checkout area.

It's terrible when you run out of room in the small self-checkout bagging area.

It's terrible that the self-checkout machine ALWAYS seems to need an attendant.

It's terrible to think that if machines really were to take over like in ***The Terminator*** that the "Era of Machines" would be short-lived due to a shortage of attendants.

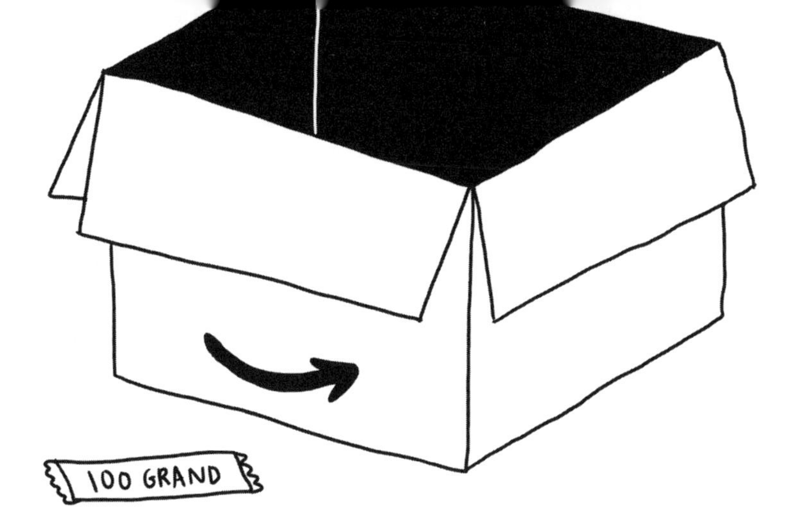

It's terrible that everything is made cheaper than it used to be.
It's terrible that nothing lasts as long as it used to.
It's terrible that everything is smaller than it used to be.
It's terrible when people end sentences in prepositions.
It's terrible that even though it's made cheaper, doesn't last as long, and is smaller…everything costs more.
It's terrible when you get less, but in bigger boxes.
It's terrible that they don't think we know…but, oh, we know!
It's terrible that they don't care that we know.

It's terrible when they raise the cost of gas for no reason.
It's terrible that the only raise I get at work is in my blood pressure.
It's terrible when tech companies slow down your tech so you have to buy an upgrade.
It's terrible that companies are still making record profits.
It's terrible that my credit card is reaching record heights.

It's terrible that they put that water pad in our meat package to make it weigh more.
It's terrible when your meat isn't as big as you were hoping.
It's terrible when people order their meat well done.
It's terrible that plant-based meat has more chemicals than real meat.
It's terrible when you say it's nice to meet you…but it's really not.

It’s terrible that it’s so hard to be a vegetarian.
It’s terrible when vegetarians are less healthy than you.
It’s terrible when restaurants serve you in Styrofoam.
It’s terrible that in some restaurants you really wish you had
a straw.
It’s terrible when you are on your last straw.

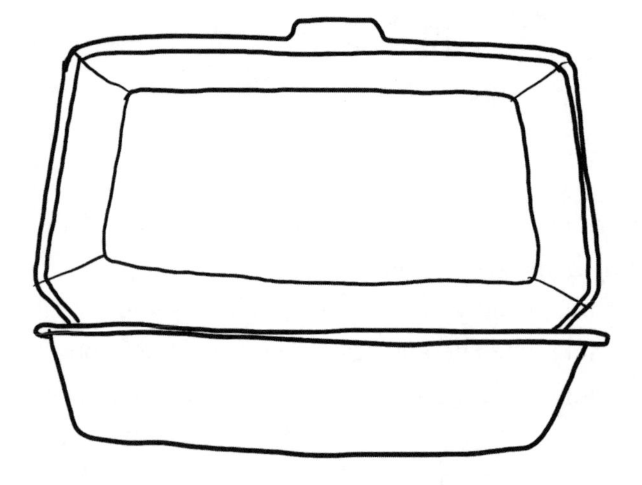

It's terrible that I have gotten blisters from trying to open those impossible-to-open blister packages.

It's terrible that if it doesn't have a five-star rating, I won't buy it.

It's terrible when big data has your targeted ads completely wrong.

It's terrible when you accidentally click on the wrong thing online and you get ads for adult diapers for the rest of time.

It's terrible that you'll know which adult diapers to get when you do need them.

It's terrible that I'd have to wait two days to get my diapers, if I really needed them.

It's terrible that I hate going out to shop.
It's terrible that it is an utter waste of a day when I don't find a package at my door.
It's terrible that our favorite retail stores are closing.
It's terrible when you have to pay for shipping.
It's terrible that I place six different online orders a day because, no matter what, all my deliveries are free!
It's terrible that nothing is really free.

CREDIT CARD STATEMENT

Switch Game $60
Hot dog costume $30
Dog's hot dog costume....... $25
Unicycle.................. $220
Nicolas Cage Banana Pillow.. $25
1,500 Ladybugs $11.08
Inflatable couch (green)..... $50
Cat Entertainment Video $6.99
Gummy Bears (2pk)........ $4.50
Full body spandex suit (red)..... $19.95
Bacon bandages............ $3.27
Pickle bathroom spray........ $5
Edible Glitter - Gold.......... $6.43

It’s terrible when it takes more than two days to get what you want in life.
It’s terrible that in two days I already forget what I ordered.
It’s terrible that most of what I buy is junk I don’t need.
It’s terrible that the more happy boxes show up at my door, the less happy I’ll be when I get my credit card statement.

It's terrible when people take up more than one parking space.

It's terrible when someone beats you to that one open parking space.

It's terrible thinking what dirty person may have touched my shopping cart last.

It's terrible thinking what diapered kid sat where I just put my veggies in the shopping cart.

It's terrible to think that someone had to change my diaper for two years.

It's terrible shopping with kids.

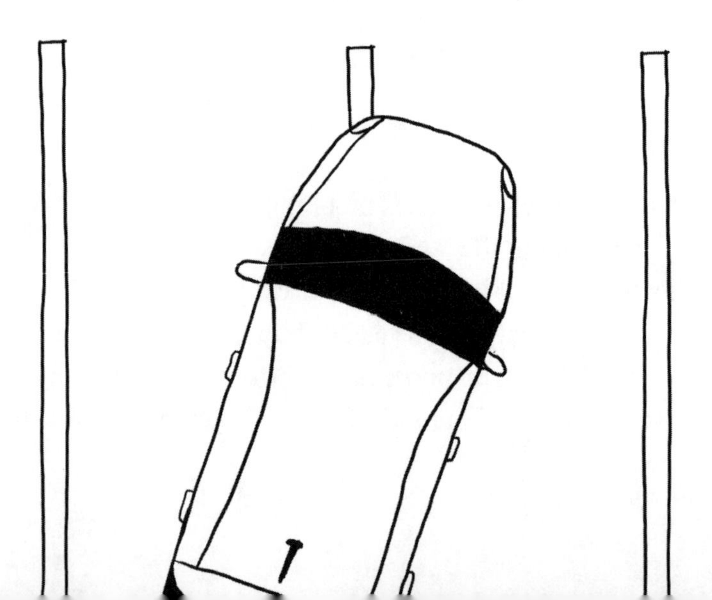

It's terrible if you've ever shopped until you dropped.
It's terrible how easily little kids drop everything.
It's terrible when a kid looks at you for a reaction if they should cry or not.

It's terrible that it feels like everyone is watching you when you buy condoms.
It's terrible that you try to get in and out of the condom aisle as fast as possible.
It's terrible when you have to buy something other than condoms in the condom aisle.
It's terrible when you feel it necessary to buy something else, like a pack of gum, whenever you buy condoms.
It's terrible if you don't even chew gum.

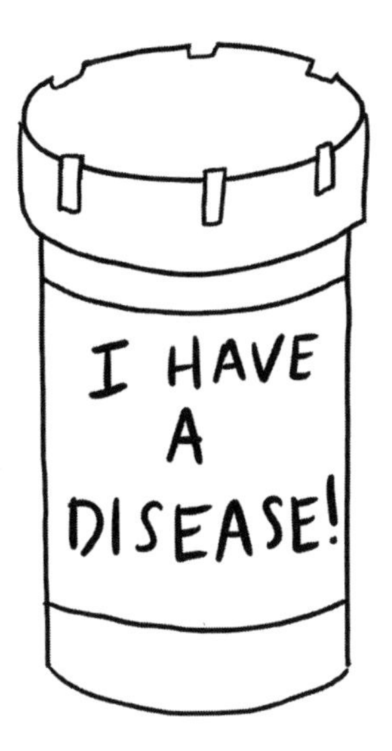

It's terrible that when you're picking up a prescription, everyone must think you have the worst disease in the world.

It's terrible when the pharmacist knows you…and your family.

It's terrible when you prematurely do the happy dance.
It's terrible when your happy dance is out of practice.
It's terrible if when dancing together, you have four left feet.
It's terrible when someone steps on your toes.
It's terrible when somebody gets to know all your moves.

It’s terrible when you become too predictable.

Oh No You Didn't!

It's terrible when people hold you back.
It's terrible when kids are off their leashes.
It's terrible that more adults aren't on leashes.

We've been told "no" or "don't" so many times in our life that it's no wonder why we're all so miserable. Throughout your life, what are all of the things that people have told you NOT to do? The list is long, I'm sure....

DON'T...

Don't... ____________________

Don't... ____________________

Don't... ____________________

Don't... ____________________

It's terrible that the more someone tells you "don't do that"...the more you want to do it.

Shoulda, Coulda, Woulda!

It's terrible when you know you should do it.
It's terrible when you don't want to do it.
It's terrible that we don't always get what we want.

Just as often as people tell you not to do something, you also have those who tell you what to do...as if they know what is best for you. Let's see all those terrible things people have said you *should* do.

YOU SHOULD...

You should... ____________________

You should... ____________________

You should... ____________________

You should... ____________________

It's terrible when you put up a long fight in not doing something you should, but in the end, when you finally did it…it actually wasn't that bad.

It’s terrible that you should take more time off…but don’t.

It’s terrible how much work it is to take time off…from work.

It’s terrible that it seems to take longer to book your vacation…than to actually enjoy it.

It’s terrible when you have to get up early for a flight…to go on vacation.

It’s terrible being in the last boarding group.

It’s terrible when you have to check your carry-on luggage.

It’s terrible when you finally forget about work on your last day of vacation.

It's terrible when your row on the plane is the only one
that's full.
It's terrible when your row is the one against the restroom
wall…that doesn't recline.
It's terrible when you suspect the person next to you didn't
put their phone in travel mode.
It's terrible that your vacation flies by, but your
uncomfortable flight home takes f o r e v e r.
It's terrible that people stand as soon as the plane lands…
even though you're not going anywhere.
It's terrible that when you land, you hear everyone's phones
ding with messages from all their friends.
It's terrible when your phone doesn't ding.

Overboard

It's terrible when other tourists end up in YOUR travel selfies.

It's terrible that no matter how hard I try when traveling… I look like a tourist.

It's terrible when you have to rush to see everything on your travels.

It's terrible when you need a vacation from your vacation.

It's a big world, and it's terrible that we won't get to see most of it, whether because we don't get enough time off or have a lack of funds, because the places are not safe destinations to go to…or because the places are fictional. On the luggage travel stickers, list some of the destinations that, sadly, you will never likely get to see.

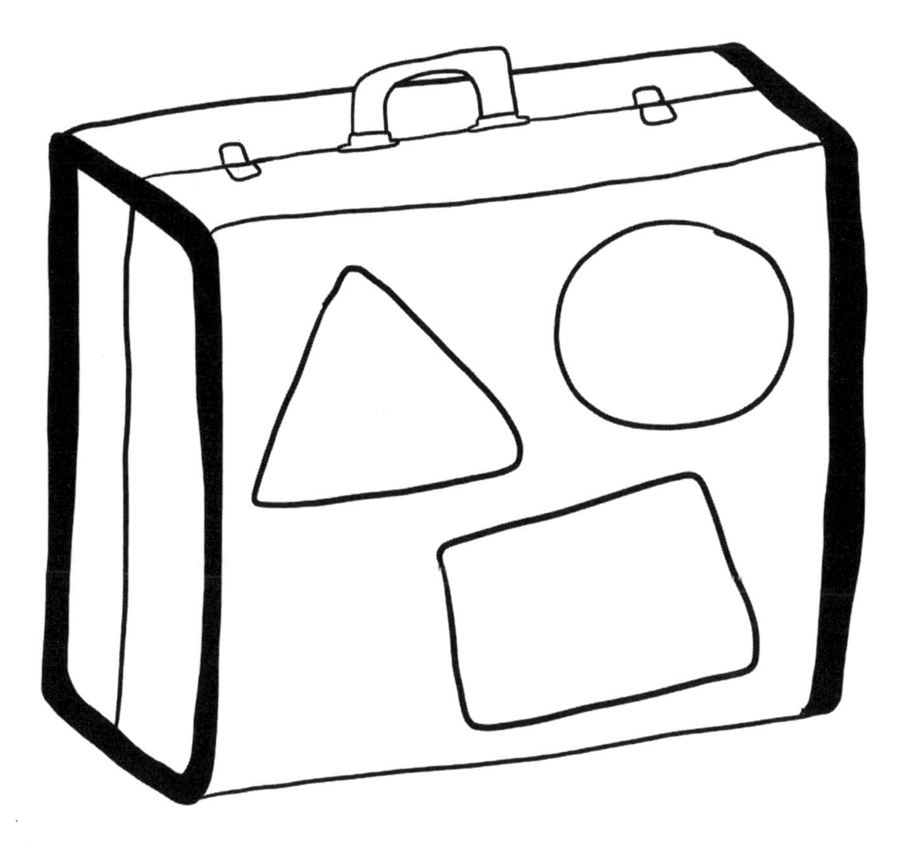

It’s terrible that we can’t travel more frequently.
It’s terrible that we can’t easily send some people away.

It's terrible how much I love spicy food.

It's terrible when your body does not love spicy food.

It's terrible if you didn't check yourself…before you wrecked yourself.

Spicy food is not for everybody. Color in the peppers here to show how much you can (or can't) tolerate spicy food.

10 Love the heat to numb my soul.

9

8

7

6

5

4

3

2

1 Spicy food is NOT for me!

It's terrible that there's nothing hot about sweating from eating.

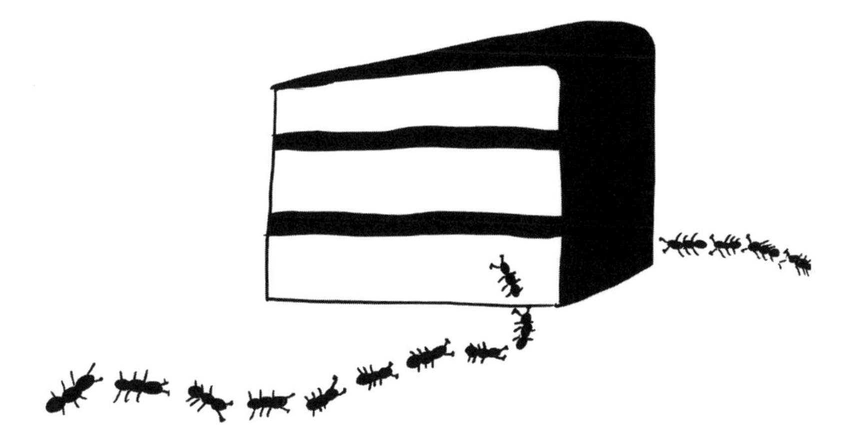

It’s terrible when there is nothing to eat.
It’s terrible when there is plenty to eat, but nothing
you want.
It’s terrible that ants can always find their way to my food.
It’s terrible that many bugs’ lives only last for days.
It’s terrible that washing my car makes it rain the next day.
It’s terrible that birds seem to use my car for target practice.
It’s terrible that practice makes perfect.
It’s terrible that nothing will ever be perfect.

It's terrible when a car loses its new car smell.
It's terrible when your hotel room smells like an ashtray.
It's terrible when you can't smell your own stink.
It's terrible when you do smell your own stink.
It's terrible when your shirt smells like stale deodorant.
It's terrible when guys wear too much cologne.
It's terrible when you sense that you are surrounded by idiots.

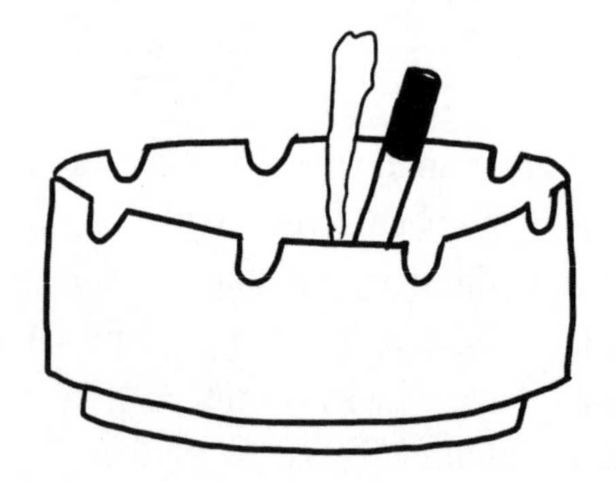

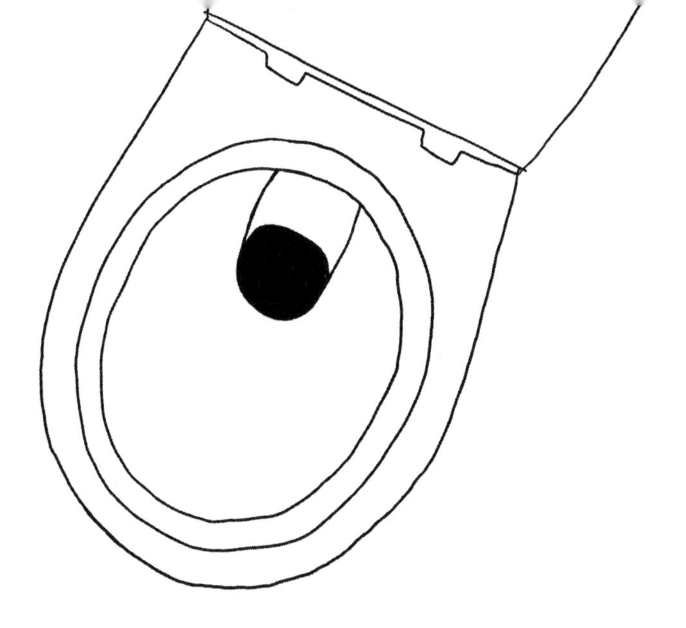

It's terrible how asparagus heightens your sense of smell
so you can smell your own stinky pee.
It's terrible when a day goes by and you haven't learned
anything new.
It's terrible that people will believe anything if you say it
with conviction.
It's terrible when you take some pleasure in messing with
people.
It's terrible when you mess with the bull, you get the horns.
It's terrible when you have to clean up somebody else's
mess.

Loser

It's terrible when you pull a bandage off slowly.
It's terrible when someone rips your bandage off fast.
It's terrible anticipating the worst.
It's terrible when the worst thing happens.

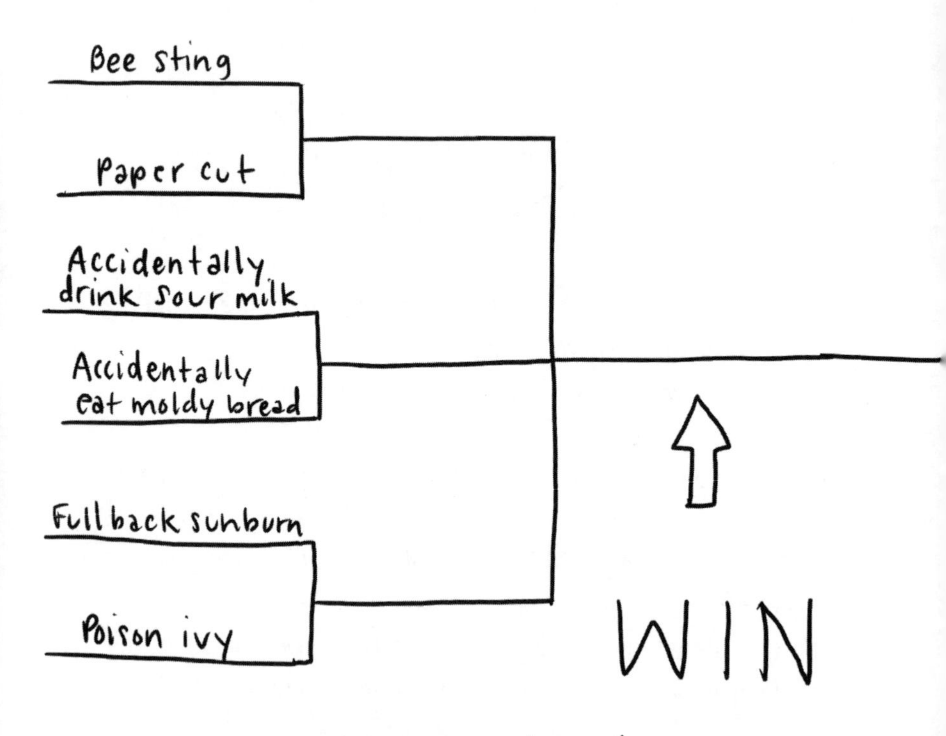

*color in the arrow of the winner

Sometimes, we are just plain unlucky and terrible things just happen. If you were in some alternate reality where you got to choose your crappy fate between lots of options, which would you ultimately choose? Take your pick in the following bracket.

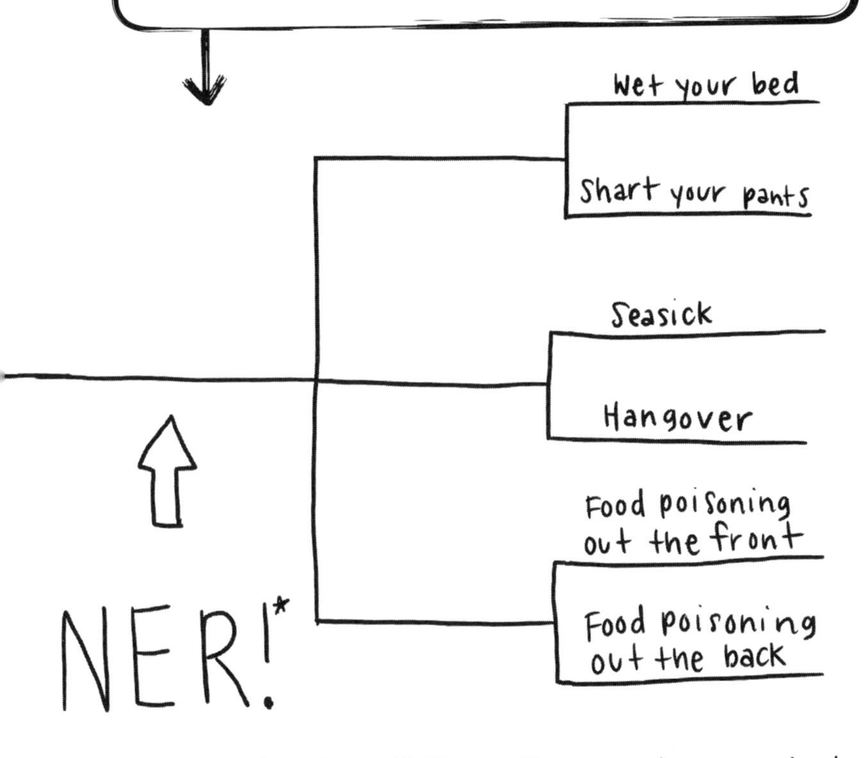

It's terrible when all the options you have are bad.

It’s terrible that your emotions can go to extremes.
It’s terrible when people mess with your emotions.
It’s terrible when people are too emotional.
It’s terrible when you can’t leave emotions out of it.
It’s terrible when they tell you to calm down.

It's terrible when people like Spock regard logic over emotions.

It's terrible that people express their emotions differently.

It's terrible if you are an introvert and don't like to share your emotions.

It's terrible when people think you can read their mind.

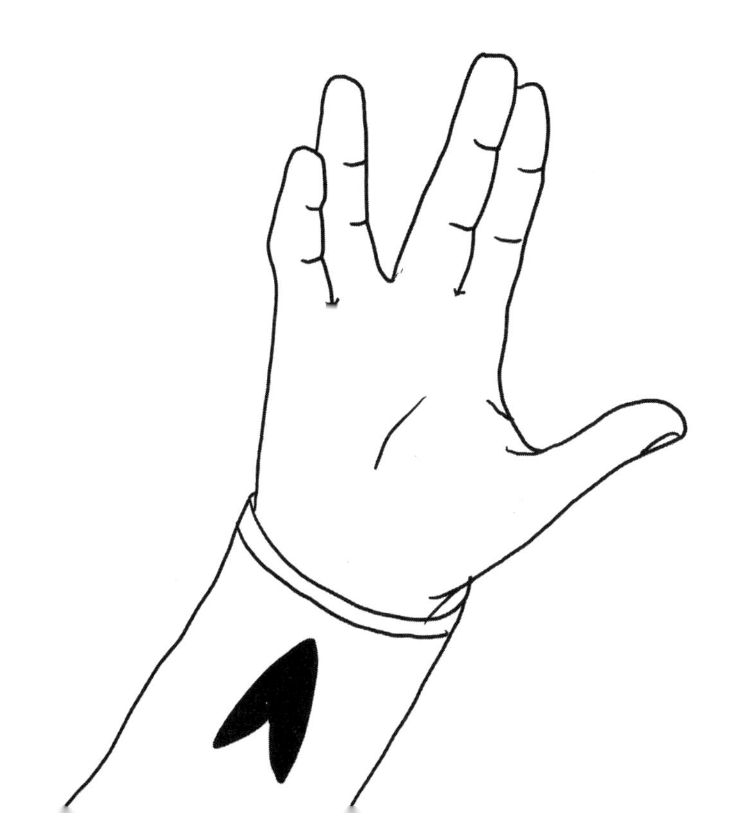

It’s terrible when people are an open book.
It’s terrible that we are still surprised by what people do.
It’s terrible that we are afraid of what some people can do.
It’s terrible when people do things intentionally to get
under our skin.
It’s terrible when terrible things make us laugh.

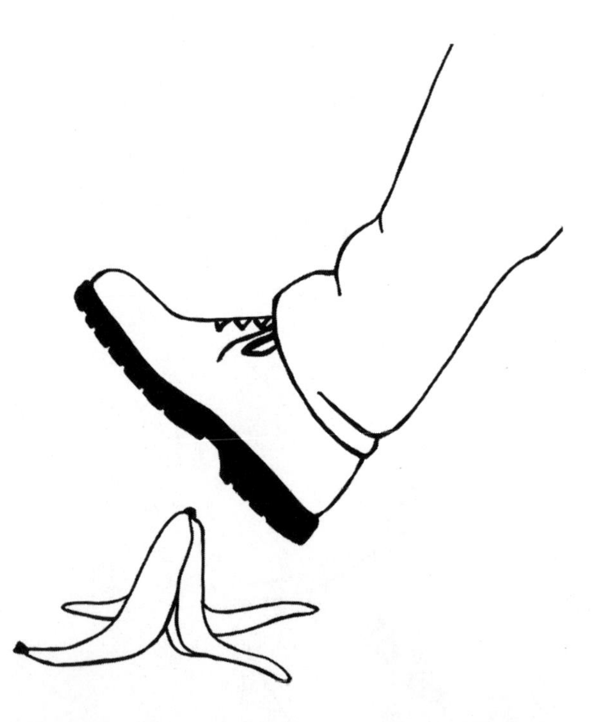

It's terrible when you are tagged in the worst pic of you ever.
It's terrible that whenever you try to use an app, it has to update first.
It's terrible when you aren't up to date.
It's terrible that with all the facial filters nobody looks like themselves anymore.
It's terrible that I don't even recognize myself without big eyes, bunny ears, and abnormally smoothed skin.

It’s terrible when someone borrows your book and dog-ears the pages.
It’s terrible when a dog bites.
It’s terrible when a bee stings.
It’s terrible that no matter what song I hear, those things are still pretty bad.

It’s terrible when people think they can sing karaoke.

It’s terrible when you realize you don’t know all the words to a song.

It’s terrible when you lose touch with who the new music artists are.

It’s terrible when they start playing your favorite songs on the oldies station.

It's terrible when you start to lose your mind.
It's terrible when you have to start over…again.
It's terrible when you didn't save a backup copy.
It's terrible when nothing can save you.
It's terrible when someone thinks they can fix you.
It's terrible when you've gotten comfortable being broken.

It's terrible when they can't fix what they broke.
It's terrible when they try to fix something that isn't broken.
It's terrible that I'm about to break.
It's terrible that most of my crayons were always broken.
It's terrible when people say the word "crowns" wrong.
It's terrible that someone always had a bigger box of
crayons.
It's terrible that my crayon pictures were never hung on
the fridge.
It's terrible that my dreams of being an artist were broken
at a young age.

Color Me Bad

It's terrible that adult coloring books seem like a lot of work.

It's terrible that I'm not good at following directions.

It's terrible that life doesn't come with directions.

It's terrible when you have the perfect vision of something in your head, and you put your heart into it, but, in the end, it just turns out to be like everything else—a waste of time and effort.

Follow the color-by-number instructions and—as you let your darkened soul release its remaining creative juices—do your best to stay within the lines.

COLOR-BY-NUMBER INSTRUCTIONS:

1 = Black 2 = Black 3 = Black 4 = Black 5 = Black

It's terrible when people
make their own rules.

Permanent Mistakes

It's ***terribul*** when ***you're*** tattoo artist has tattoos spelled wrong.

It's terrible that tattoos don't stand the test of time.

Tattoos are the ultimate means of expression, but some people make bad decisions when it comes to their tattoos, and they are stuck with them for the rest of their life. On the person outline on the next page, draw the worst ideas for tattoos.

It's terrible that tattoos are as addictive as Oreos. I already have _______ tattoo(s)!

It's terrible when it hurts more to remove a person's tattooed name than to remove them.

It's terrible that there isn't an undo button on life.

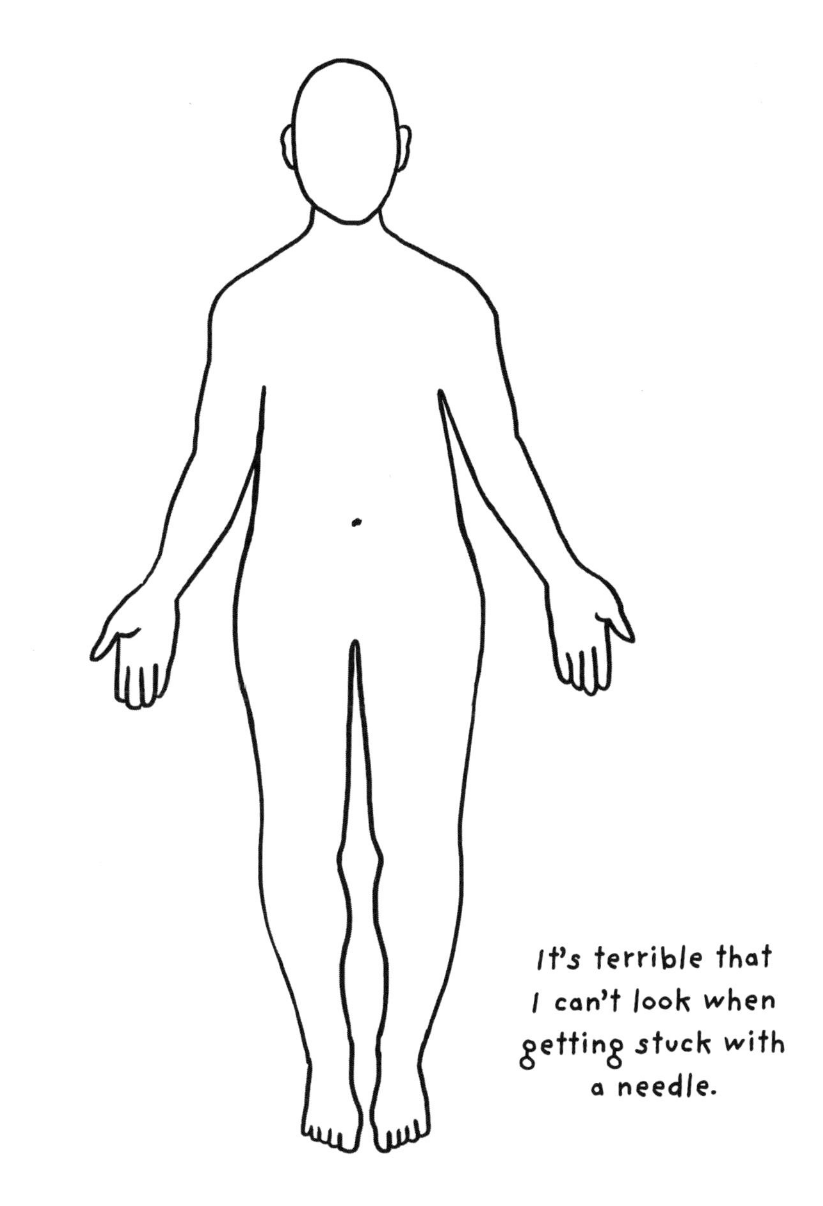
It's terrible that
I can't look when
getting stuck with
a needle.

Little Things

It's terrible when ALL of your underwear is in the hamper.
It's terrible when you've chipped a nail.
It's terrible when the sink is full of dishes.
It's terrible when your car is 5,000 miles past its oil change.
It's terrible when your favorite shirt gets a hole.
It's terrible when your fish is out of food.
It's terrible when you don't know where that smell is coming from.

It's terrible that we waste our time stressing over insignificant little things.
It's terrible that when there are so many little things, like raindrops hitting you all at once, it feels like a tidal wave.

In and around each little raindrop, quickly jot down all the little things that add up and make you feel like you are drowning.

It's terrible when it's
quantity over quality.

It's terrible when the
light at the end of the tunnel
is a train coming right at you.

It's terrible when you wake up after a night of partying and feel like you've been hit by a train.

It's terrible when at work they say, "We need a backup in case you are ever hit by a bus."

It's terrible when the "bus option" to get out of work… doesn't sound so bad.

It's terrible that fares keep going up.
It's terrible when the number on the scale doesn't go down.
It's terrible when you can't get a seat on the train.
It's terrible when you don't want to hold the dirty handrail...***for your own safety***.
It's terrible if you are a germaphobe in this dirty world.

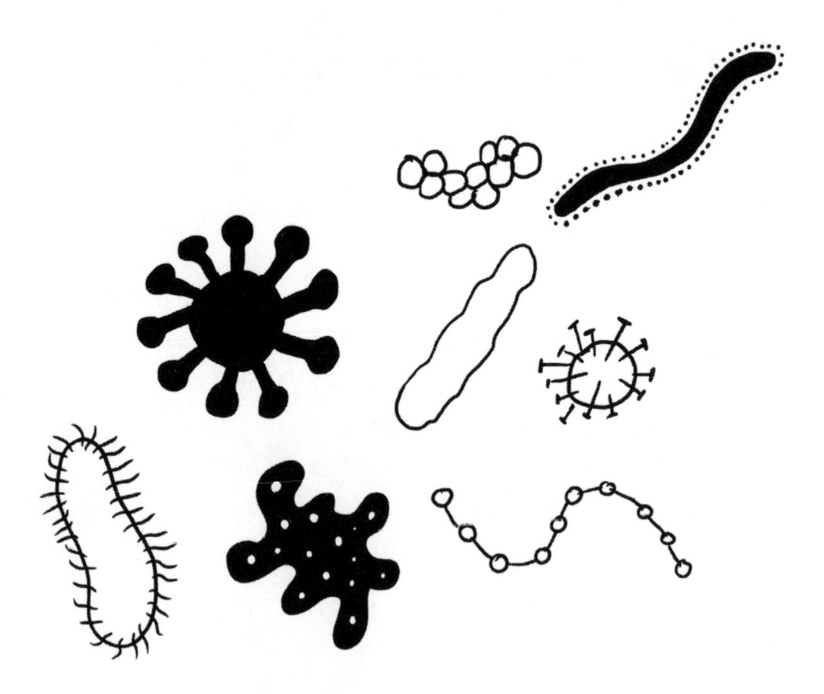

It's terrible that dirty is hot, but filthy is dirty.
It's terrible when the lines are blurred.
It's terrible when you get new glasses and realize
how much you didn't see.
It's terrible that we don't stop and look around.

Emergency Exit

It's über-terrible when your Uber driver turns out to be someone you know.

It's über-terrible when your Uber driver is more invested in a conversation with you than in driving.

It's über-terrible when your Uber driver is too old to be driving.

It's über-terrible when you both know it was your Uber driver who farted.

It's über-terrible when your return home Uber driver is the same person you just gave a bad review to on your way out.

It's über-terrible when your Uber driver is also your date.

It's über-terrible when your Uber ride cancels when they see you.

People are notorious for giving bad excuses to get out of situations. Write down some of the worst excuses you could give—or that you have received—to get out of something.

3:24PM
Hey um, I'm really sorry I won't be able to make it because...

It’s terrible when someone moves your car seat and mirrors.
It’s terrible when it’s because you needed them to drive you
home.
It’s terrible when you wake up and don’t know where
you are.
It’s terrible when you wake up and don’t want to be
where you are.
It’s terrible when your life isn’t going where you want
it to go.
It’s terrible when you’re not going anywhere, fast.
It’s terrible when you have to let it go…let it go.…
It’s terrible when you are frozen in your path.

It's terrible if you complain about where you live.

It's terrible when you have to move.

It's terrible when very little will get you moving.

It's terrible when you've hit your ceiling.

It's terrible when the roof, the roof, the roof is on fire.

It's terrible when things get heated.

It's terrible when things got steamy with your parents…and you accidentally walked in.

It's terrible when you can't unsee things.

Mantra

It's terrible when you have the best idea ever in the middle of the night and forget come morning.
It's terrible when practice doesn't make perfect.
It's terrible that no matter how many times I repeat someone's name, I still forget it.

Everything in this world has gotten so terrible that we often find ourselves muttering little phrases under our breath, like, "Screw everyone," or "F this place!" In a way, these have become our personal mantras. Repeat your favorite terrible mantra again and again and again in the space provided.

It's terrible when people repeat themselves.

It’s terrible that your plants don’t remind you to water them.

It’s terrible that I’m only happy when it rains.

It’s terrible that I don’t have a green thumb.

It’s terrible that I’m not sure how I keep myself alive.

It’s terrible when you see a fire truck or ambulance going somewhere.

It’s terrible if you get right behind a fire truck or ambulance because you know it’ll cut through all the traffic.

It’s terrible when someone cuts you off.

It’s terrible when the bartender cuts you off.

It’s terrible when you can’t cut right through all the BS.

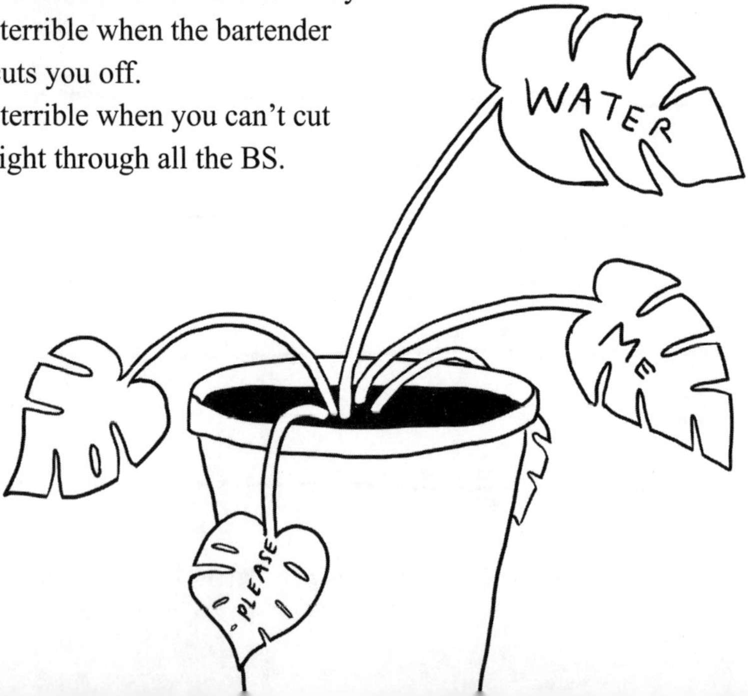

It’s terrible when they want to go Dutch.
It’s terrible when your mom or dad would not approve.
It’s terrible when someone wants to set you up on a date.
It’s terrible when you look for love too hard.
It’s terrible when you fall too hard.
It’s terrible when they fall too quickly.
It’s terrible when your backup plan falls for someone else.

TRUTH

It's terrible when people stretch the truth on their dating profile.
It's terrible when they all-out lie on their dating profile.
It's terrible when they save the big bomb for your fifth date.
It's terrible when there is no second date.
It's terrible when there are plenty of fish in the sea…but there is something fishy about the ones who are left.

It's terrible that a first kiss is so awkward.

It's terrible if you say I love you first, and they don't say it back.

It's terrible if they say I love you first, and you say thank you.

It's terrible when you kiss someone good morning before they've brushed their teeth.

It's terrible when you accidentally use someone else's toothbrush.

It's terrible that you've likely done a lot worse, but that really grosses you out.

It's terrible when the person you fell in love with starts getting comfortable in gross ways.

It’s terrible if you never got to play spin the bottle.
It’s terrible when they have their eyes on someone else.
It’s terrible when you are caught looking.
It’s terrible that I developed late.
It’s terrible that I’m still immature.

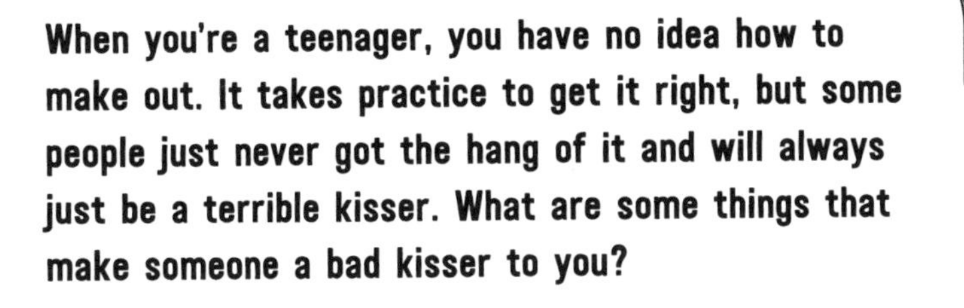

When you're a teenager, you have no idea how to make out. It takes practice to get it right, but some people just never got the hang of it and will always just be a terrible kisser. What are some things that make someone a bad kisser to you?

It's terrible when you'd rather be kissing someone else.

It's terrible when you get tongue-tied around someone you are attracted to.
It's terrible that you only have one chance to make a good first impression.
It's terrible when you don't have a chance.
It's terrible when you don't take a chance.
It's terrible when your chances are one in a million.
It's terrible when all you've heard is that there is a chance.

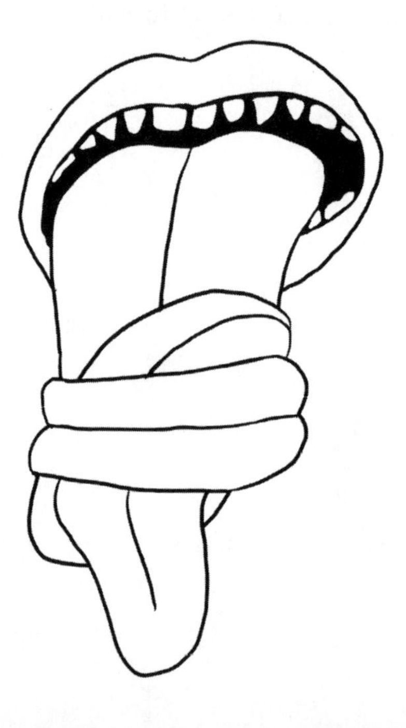

109

110...

112

113...

ugh

It's terrible that we seldom get second chances.

It's terrible when people say, "This will just take a second."

It's terrible when you lose count.

It's terrible when you're just a number.

Far from Perfect

It's terrible that I'll never date a perfect 10.
It's terrible when I see others who land people who are out of their range.
It's terrible that I'll never have a perfect body.
It's terrible that some people do have perfect bodies.
It's terrible that nobody seems happy with their body.

We all have things that we don't like about ourselves, *and* we have some terrible personality traits that we think others don't like about us. Above the sculpture of "The Thinker," create a list of the top terrible things from both perspectives.

→

Things I don't like about myself
Things I think other people don't like about me
It's terrible when others think they are perfect.

It’s terrible that it takes 102 pics to get the perfect selfie.

It’s terrible when you can’t figure out which pic in your photo library to use.

It's terrible when someone offers to take your picture for you, and they couldn't have taken a worse pic.
It's terrible when you are the one who takes all the pictures…and you aren't in any of them.
It's terrible when you feel like you don't exist.

It's terrible that we get so little recognition for a job well done.

It's terrible when people expect to get recognition for what they get paid to do.

It's terrible when you spend your whole paycheck because you get a discount where you work.

It's terrible when rewards programs cost us.

It's terrible that I have so many rewards cards they need their own wallet.

It's terrible when you can't find the rewards card you want to use.

It's terrible that I've never cashed in on a rewards program.

It's terrible when someone sends you money via an app you don't have.

It's terrible when you reach the age that birthday cards no longer come with money.

It's terrible that the $5 that Nana and Poppy used to send wouldn't even buy a coffee today.

It's terrible that $5 can still buy a precooked rotisserie chicken.

Everything has gotten so expensive. What would you possibly buy with your $5 (that's not a rotisserie chicken)?

____

It's terrible that I'm not as thrifty with money as Nana and Poppy.

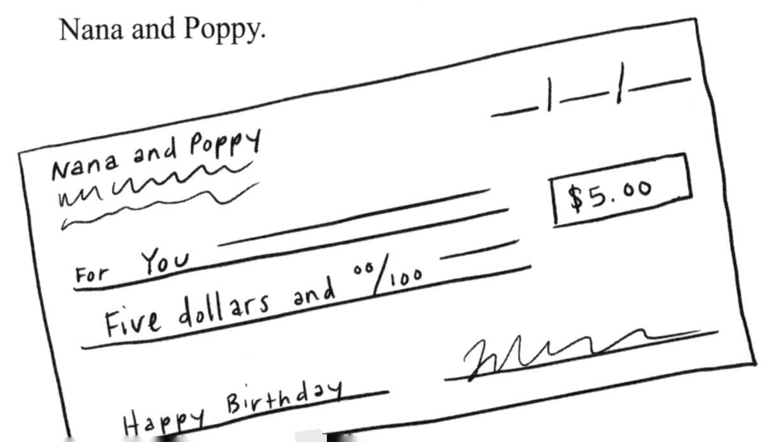

Material World

It's terrible that we live in a material world.
It's terrible that I want lots of stuff.
It's terrible that everything I want is expensive.
It's terrible that diamonds are a girl's best friend.
It's terrible that we don't appreciate what we have…until it's gone.

There are few material possessions that we cherish in this world. Answer the following questions about the ones you may cherish (or desire) the most:

1. What is the one materialistic possession that would be terrible if you lost it?

2. What is the one superficial possession that you no longer have and wish you did?

3. Why do you no longer have that possession?

4. What is the one material item that you'll never possess?

5. Name one person who you are pretty sure is possessed.

It's terrible when people go off track.

It's terrible when you have champagne taste on a beer budget.

It's terrible that you are able to make your money last a lot longer when you are younger.

It's terrible that you are able to last a lot longer on just about everything when you are younger.

It's terrible that sugary cereal doesn't taste as good as I remember.

It's terrible when you are exposed to the finer things.

It's terrible when you don't know which fork you are supposed to use.

It's terrible that nobody really knows which fork you are supposed to use.

It’s terrible when you are cooking for people and don’t know if the food is really done.
It’s terrible when you look in your fridge and the food was done a long time ago.
It’s terrible that we don’t know our own expiration dates.

It's terrible to have to go through all that effort to cook for just yourself.
It's terrible when you don't want to go out to eat and be at a table for one.
It's terrible that if you don't go out, you will always be alone.
It's terrible that dating is a lot like food:

- If it is fuzzy…
- If it smells or tastes bad…
- If it's soft and oozy…
- If the meat is gray…

…you don't want it, no matter how hungry you are.

It's terrible when they leave it open.
It's terrible when they leave it out.
It could be terrible when you drink milk past its
expiration date.
It's terrible when you defy the odds.
It's terrible when you push your luck.

Stanky

It's terrible when someone belches and you know what they had for lunch.
It's terrible when someone has tooted in the elevator before you enter.
It's terrible when you have to naively pretend it wasn't you who accidentally has passed gas.
It's terrible when you have to sniff your own armpits to see if that smell is you.

There are a lot of disgusting things that we experience in our lives, but not much is worse than when a smell makes you gag. This reflex can be different for everyone, but what are the top 10 most pungently disgusting, worst, smelliest things to YOU?!

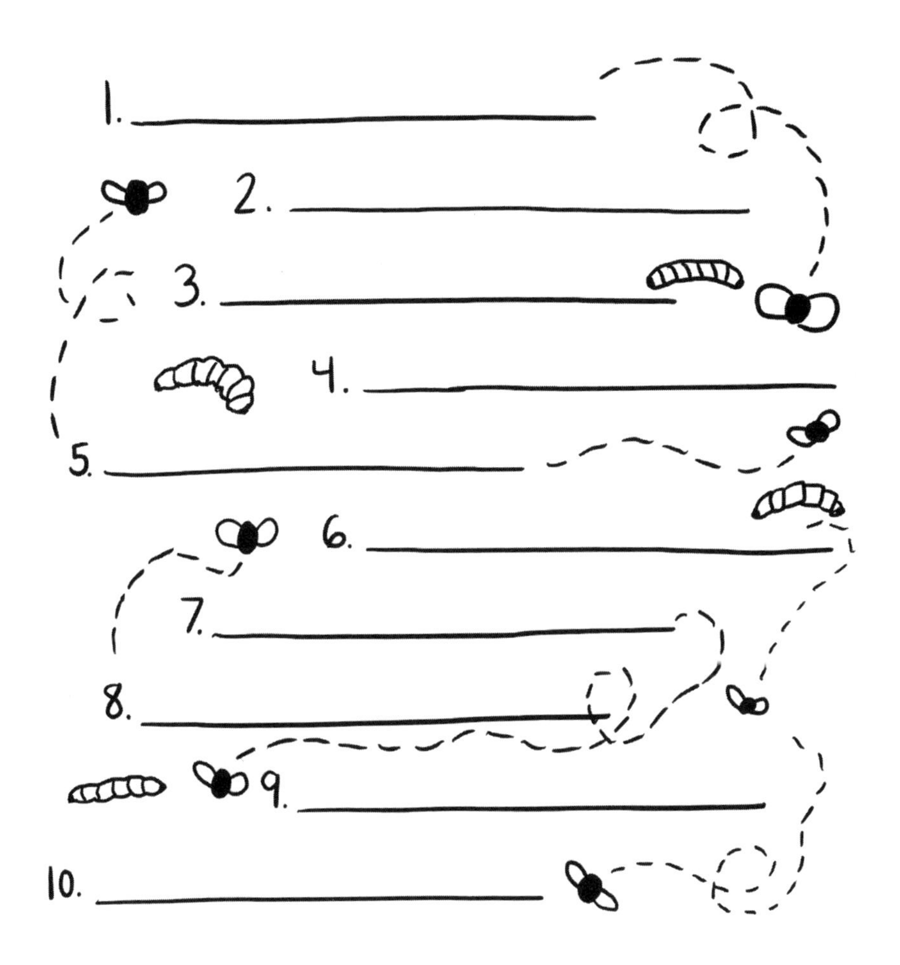

It’s terrible when you can smell someone’s BS.

It's terrible when you have to open up a can of whoop ass.
It's terrible when you've opened a can of worms.
It's terrible when you can't contain yourself.
It's terrible when you really have ***to*** go.
It's terrible when there's ***a*** line for the bathroom.
It's terrible when ***it's*** too late.
It's terrible when they put the emphasis on ***the*** wrong word.
It's terrible ***when you can't emphasize something enough***.

It's terrible that nobody really understands.
It's terrible when you don't understand.
It's terrible when there is a misunderstanding.
It's terrible when you are misunderstood.
It's terrible when you are stood up.
It's terrible when you don't stand up for what you believe in.

It's terrible if you are the tallest person in the room.
It's terrible when everyone is taller than you.

It's terrible when you can't reach anything.
It's terrible when you have to reach everything for
everyone.

It's terrible when you don't mean to look down on
everyone.
It's terrible when you have to look up to someone you
don't look up to.

It's terrible that only short or tall people really understand
these problems.

It’s terrible when you can’t see what’s under the water.
It’s terrible when something touches you while swimming.
It’s terrible that whatever touched you is likely more
freaked out…that you touched it.

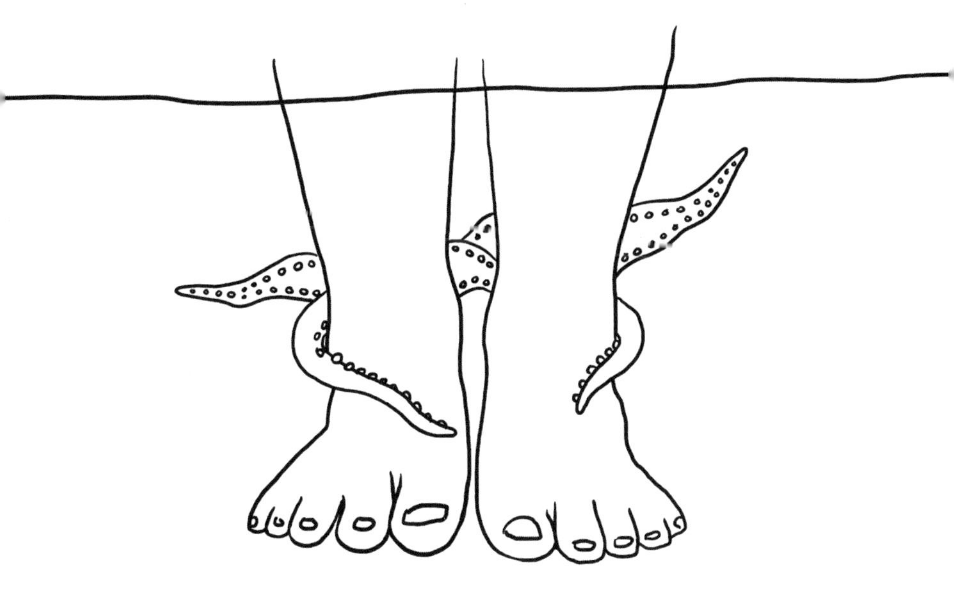

It's terrible that I don't understand why fish tanks are so much work when it's just…water, fish, food.

It's terrible that in return, all they do for you is just swim back and forth all day.

It would be terrible if someone tapped on your home and stared at you with their big head, waiting for you to do something.

It’s terrible when everything must stop until that guy checks
their microbrews into their app.
It’s terrible that of all things, beer has produced snobs.
It’s terrible when anyone voices their unwanted opinion.
It’s terrible that we all can’t get along.
It’s terrible when someone has to have the last word.

It’s terrible when I told you so.

It's terrible that when I'm quiet...

...it's because I have nothing nice to say.

It’s terrible when you just need some peace and quiet.
It’s terrible when silence is music to your ears.
It’s terrible when people don’t just shut up and listen.
It’s terrible when people tell you how much they love
peace and quiet.

It's terrible when you have
to speak in public.
It's terrible if you had to be
something insignificant like
a tree in your school play.
It's terrible if you have to go see a school play.
It's terrible that little kids don't play outside anymore.
It's terrible when the air is fresher inside.
It's terrible when you smash a bug and hear it crunch.
It's terrible when your food gets soggy.
It's terrible when someone shakes your hand with wet
hands.

It’s terrible when you want to run away.
It’s terrible when you have no place to go.

It’s terrible when you can just scream.
It’s terrible that nobody cares to listen.

It’s terrible when you are just done.
It’s terrible when they aren’t finished with you.

It’s terrible when you want to give up.
It’s terrible when you have nothing left to give.

It’s terrible when it’s only Monday.

It's terrible that we like people to serve us.
It's terrible when there is no service.
It's terrible when there are plenty of people to serve you,
but nobody will.
It's terrible when you are served.
It's terrible when you get in trouble.
It's terrible when it's not your fault.
It's terrible when you have no excuse.

It's terrible when the people who are the closest get there last.

It's terrible when people take four times longer than you to get ready to go.

It's terrible that you are never going to be 100% ready for whatever's next.

It's terrible when people put 0% effort into looking presentable.

It's terrible when people wear pajamas in public.

It's terrible if you can't remember the last time you've had a good nap.

It's terrible that we no longer get to sleep in as late
as we want.
It's terrible that we no longer get a recess period.
It's terrible that we no longer get food prepared for us.
It's terrible that we no longer stick to an early bedtime.
It's terrible that we wanted to hurry and grow up.

It's terrible that we had to go out and find our own friends as kids instead of having playdates arranged for us.

It's terrible that kids' social calendars are more booked up than ours.

It's terrible when young kids give you that smug, inquisitive look as if they are judging you.

It's terrible when you question who is in charge.

Su	M	Tu	W	Th	F	Sa
	last night of Little League		Soccer 6pm		piano recital	play date w/ Taylor
Marshall Bday 3pm			Soccer 6pm	cupcakes 4 class	Sleepover w/ Adam	Jack Bday 1pm
		Movie w/ Smiths	Soccer 6pm		Pizza night!	
Group Science project			Soccer 6PM	Aquarium Field trip		Basket ball tryouts

It's terrible that you are only young once.

It's terrible that you don't appreciate your youth while you have it.

It's terrible that as you get older, your mind says, "Yes," but your body says, "What the hell are you thinking?"

It's terrible when you still feel young, but the mirror says otherwise.

It's only going to get worse from here. What are 3 things you dread will suck even more the older you get?

1. ______________________________

2. ______________________________

3 ______________________________

It's terrible when the person in the mirror doesn't smile back.

It was terrible when you were in that awkward transitional stage in life.

It's terrible if you are still in an awkward stage in your life.

It's terrible when you awkwardly use scissors made for the other hand.

It's terrible when it's all hands on deck.

It's terrible when you have to get your hands dirty.

It's terrible when you have your hands full.

It's terrible when you know firsthand.

It's terrible when they get the upper hand.

It's terrible when you overplay your hand.

It's terrible when it's a losing battle.
It's terrible when all they want to do is fight.
It's terrible when the bigger they are, the harder you fall.
It's terrible if you are not very big.
It's terrible that there is a time and place where size matters.

It's terrible when you have to wait 90 minutes for a 90-second amusement park ride.
It's terrible that everywhere can't be the most magical place on Earth.
It's terrible how much it costs to enjoy the magic of Disney.
It's terrible that people bring their kids to Disney.
It's terrible that I'm just a big kid.

It's terrible when you lose the magic.

It's terrible when you see a bad magician.

It's terrible that there are no such things as magic wands.

It's terrible that unicorns no longer exist.

It's terrible that real life never sends you on magical quests.

It's terrible when you come home with glitter on your face and you don't know where it came from…or how long it's been there.

It's terrible if you'd be better suited as a villain than a prince or princess.

Villains are usually up to no good, but sometimes the bad guys are kinda cool. Time to fess up: Which villain have you rooted for?

It's terrible that I feel like I would actually embrace having a lair.

It would be terrible to be a villain's sidekick.

It's terrible that villains foolishly reveal their sinister master plan to their captured hero.

It's terrible that bad guys laugh.

It's terrible when you hear a real person with an evil laugh.

Superbad

It's terrible that I'm really not good at anything.
It's terrible that I'm actually super bad at most things.
It's terrible when people are super talented and waste it.
It's terrible that superheroes have to wear tights.
It's terrible that superheroes keep their identities a secret.

Perhaps there is a reason why superheroes keep their identities a secret. If I had superpowers, it's terrible that I would likely use them for no good. What superpowers would you want to have, and how would you use them for your own selfish reasons?

MY SUPER POWERS
& THE TERRIBLE THINGS I'D DO WITH THEM...
It's terrible that it's fun to be bad.
It's terrible that capes aren't more in fashion.

Bad Places

It would be terrible to be eaten by a zombie.
It's terrible when no condiment makes your food taste better.
It would be terrible to be a zombie and have to eat people.
It's terrible that I'm already always hungry.

In all those fictional stories, having a villain is bad, but it's worse when the whole world, land, or place where they wreak their havoc is also terrible. Document the worst, most horrid fictional settings and note which location takes the prize as the "MOST DREADFUL PLACE OF THEM ALL."

It's terrible that only the strong survive.

It's terrible that all the cool stuff *happened* a long time ago, in a galaxy *far, far away.*

It's terrible when your father strikes *down your* elderly mentor.

It's terrible when your father cuts off *your hand.*

It's terrible when you find out your father *is the bad guy.*

It's terrible when they don't know the difference between Star Wars and Star Trek.

It's terrible if you are in a relationship with someone who prefers the opposite franchise.

Whether you are a Trekkie of any generation or someone who is strong in the Force...if you prefer one sci-fi series over the other, you are the enemy of the other series' fans.

Let's see whose sh*t list you are on. Estimate how many of each franchise's movies you've seen at least once.

Star Wars: ____________________

Star Trek: ____________________

If both are zero, then you are on the sh*t list of all sci-fi fans.

No matter what, it's terrible if you don't love Baby Yoda.

Deal Breakers

It's terrible that we set our standards so high.
It's terrible that beggars can't be choosers.
It's terrible when people settle.
It's terrible that I've settled for a lot less.

The likelihood of finding someone who will meet all of your criteria is very, very thin. Some things you can tolerate, but there are a few deal breakers that you just can't get past, no matter how hot or perfect they might be otherwise.

What are the terrible deal breakers that will always make you move on from a relationship with someone?

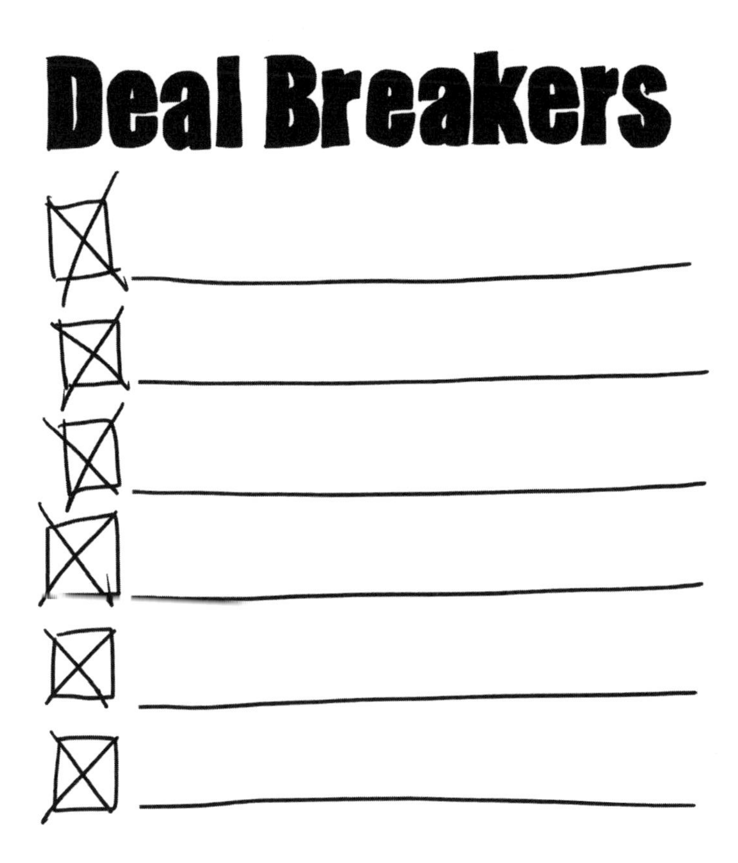

It's terrible that someone has to deal with all of my flaws.

Selfish Vices

It's terrible when someone puts their needs ahead of yours.
It's terrible when you need it versus want it.
It's terrible when you want it and can't get it.
It's terrible when you can get what you want too easily.
It's terrible when you want it all.

There are important things in people's lives, like love, family, health, laughter, blah, blah, blah. But then, there are vices that we really get into...maybe a little too much.

Draw an X over all but your top 3 selfish vices. There is an open space for you to add one more of your own. Then draw a circle around the one vice you wouldn't be able to survive this terrible world without.

CAFFEINE	SALON	SMOKING
ALCOHOL	FOOD	MUSIC/ TV/ GAMES
SEX	TRAVEL	SHOPPING
MASSAGE	SLEEP	

It's terrible when you have to choose between
more than one love.

It's terrible when the Tupperware lids don't match.
It's terrible when you've met your match.
It's terrible when your sock loses its match.
It's terrible when you have a pile of lonely socks that will never have a match again.
It's terrible when a sock quits on you.
It's terrible when your parents quit folding your laundry for you.
It's terrible that I still can't fold my laundry as good as my mom.
It's terrible that I quit folding my laundry too.
It's terrible that now none of my socks match.

It's terrible when you can't quit.
It's terrible when you don't want to quit.
It's terrible when you have to quit.
It's terrible when they quit on you.
It's terrible that we don't learn from our mistakes.
It's terrible when quitting was the better option.
It's terrible that we're dumb enough to do it again.
It's terrible that we're taught not to be quitters.

Bad Habits

It's terrible that things that are bad for us…are enjoyable.
It's terrible that bad things are habitual.
It's terrible that bad habits are hard to break.
It's terrible that there are no good habits.

We all have them, those pesky habits that you know you should stop doing or people always remind you that you should quit. We know we're not strong enough to quit, at least for long, so in the bar graph, label and rate your worst of the worst habits.

It's terrible when you are good at something that isn't good for you.

It's terrible when life is like a box of chocolates…and you don't know what you are going to get.

It's terrible when you do know what you are going to get.

It's terrible when you deserve what you are going to get.

It's terrible that, when the going gets tough…

…the tough get going…

…but you are not tough…

…and you're not going anywhere.

It's terrible when anything is possible.
It's terrible that "the world is your oyster" makes no sense.
It would be terrible to be an oyster.
It's terrible that there is always room for improvement.
It's terrible that I'm far from perfect.
It's terrible that I am always right.
It's terrible when I have to repeat myself.
It's terrible when I have to repeat myself.

It’s terrible when they know you’re coming, but they don’t hold the door.

It’s terrible when you think they ***might’ve*** actually pushed the “close elevator door” button.

It’s terrible when there is plenty of room, but nobody moves in.

It’s terrible when the elevator stops, and nobody gets off.

It’s terrible when someone interrupts you.

It's terrible when there is only one last button to push.
It's terrible who might have access to that button.
It's terrible when you don't know what a button does.

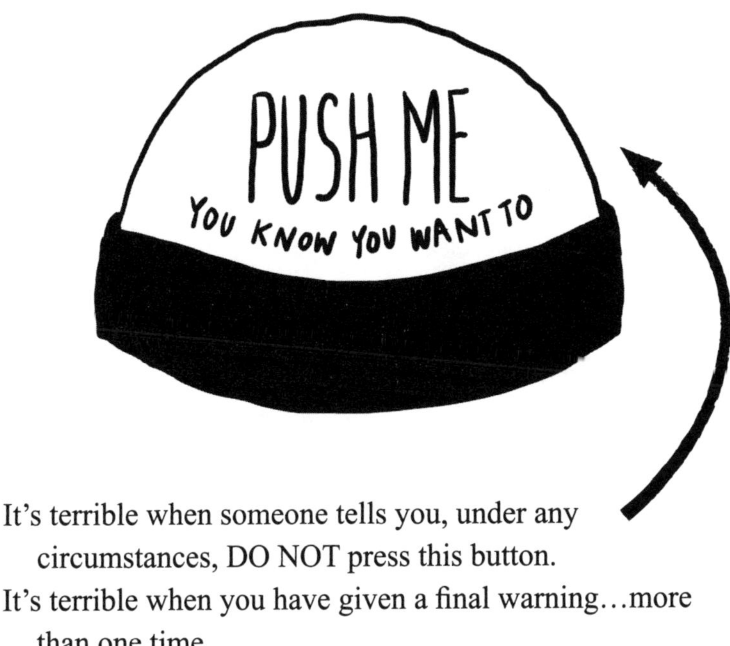

It's terrible when someone tells you, under any circumstances, DO NOT press this button.
It's terrible when you have given a final warning…more than one time.

DEFCON 1

It's terrible when someone borrows something, and you have to ask for it back—again.
It's terrible when someone returns something they've borrowed…and it's broken.
It's terrible when you lose your cool.
It's terrible when someone tells you to just take a deep breath.

Sooner or later we all reach our breaking point and totally lose our cool. Whatever happened may not have warranted an explosion by itself, but when we have had enough, we can't help exploding.

What are some of those terrible things that just keep happening over and over and have either made you crack or would make you lose it if they happen one more time?

It's terrible when you have nobody to explode on.

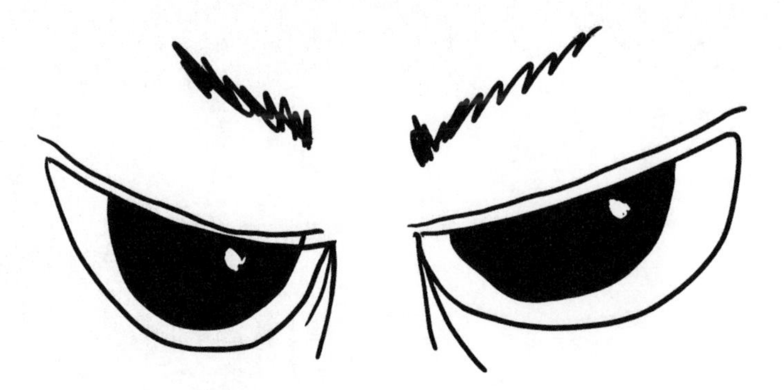

It's terrible when you can't express yourself the way you want to.
It's terrible when there is no express lane.
It's terrible when the expression on their face says it all.
It's terrible when it's nothing like you expected.
It's terrible when you've given it your all.

It’s terrible when you can’t find the energy to exercise.
It’s terrible that I don’t like to run.
It’s terrible that I always seem to be running somewhere.
It’s terrible that I can’t seem to slow down.
It’s terrible that life is passing me by.
It’s terrible that the best is yet to come.
It’s terrible if the best has already come…and went.

Ticking Away

It's terrible how quickly time flies by…except when you are at work.

It's terrible that I always wait until the last minute.

It's terrible that my list keeps getting longer, but nothing comes off it.

It's terrible that I don't know where all the time went.

It's terrible how much time we truly waste, but we have nothing to show for it.

Let's make a pie chart to see where all of your time goes! Start by coloring in the options (and add some of your own if needed). Then use the color codes to make your personal pie chart. Be sure to fill the pie in to 100% for all the time that is wasted.

It's terrible if all you got out of this exercise is that you want pie.

Lack of Talent

It's terrible when you love to sing, but…only sing when alone in the car.

It's terrible when you love to dance, but…don't dare dance in public.

It's terrible that you'd love to play an instrument, but…will never take lessons.

It's terrible when you haven't found your talent yet.

There are a lot of talented people in this world, and, personally, I'm a little jealous of those lucky SOBs. Everyone dreams of having some amazing talent, but I'm just lousy at most things I try.

If there was a section on a resume for your worst skills, what are those things that you are exceptionally bad at…and likely will never be good at doing?

— Resume —

My Name:

My Current Role:

My Worst Skills:

It's terrible that I've never come across a listing for a dream job.

It's terrible that we spend our prime years prepping for what we will do for the rest of our lives.

It's terrible that we'd live more if we didn't have to work every day.

It's terrible that by the time we're able to retire, we won't be able to physically do the things that we want to do now.

It's terrible when you are exhausted just by thinking about work.

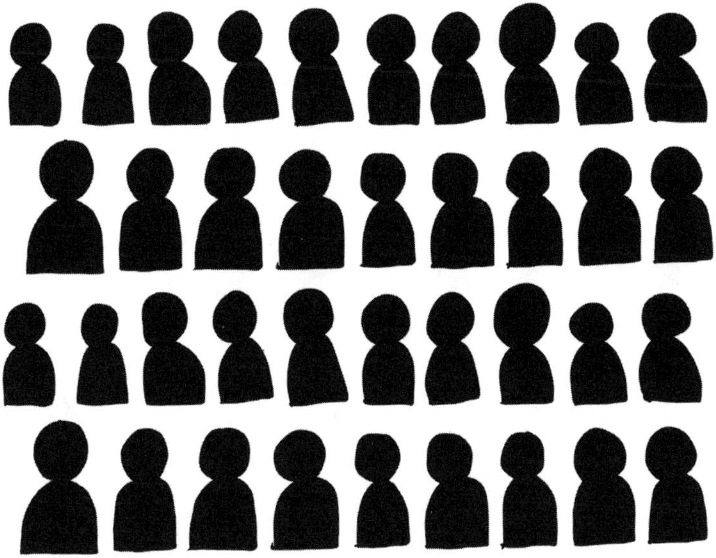

It’s terrible that I feel I’m irreplaceable at my job.
It’s terrible that I’m underpaid for what I do at my job.
It’s terrible that they would not only replace me, but also pay the next person more.
It’s terrible that when they replace me, they would also blame everything wrong on me.
It’s terrible that I can’t find a better job to replace this terrible job…because all jobs are terrible.

Dentists.

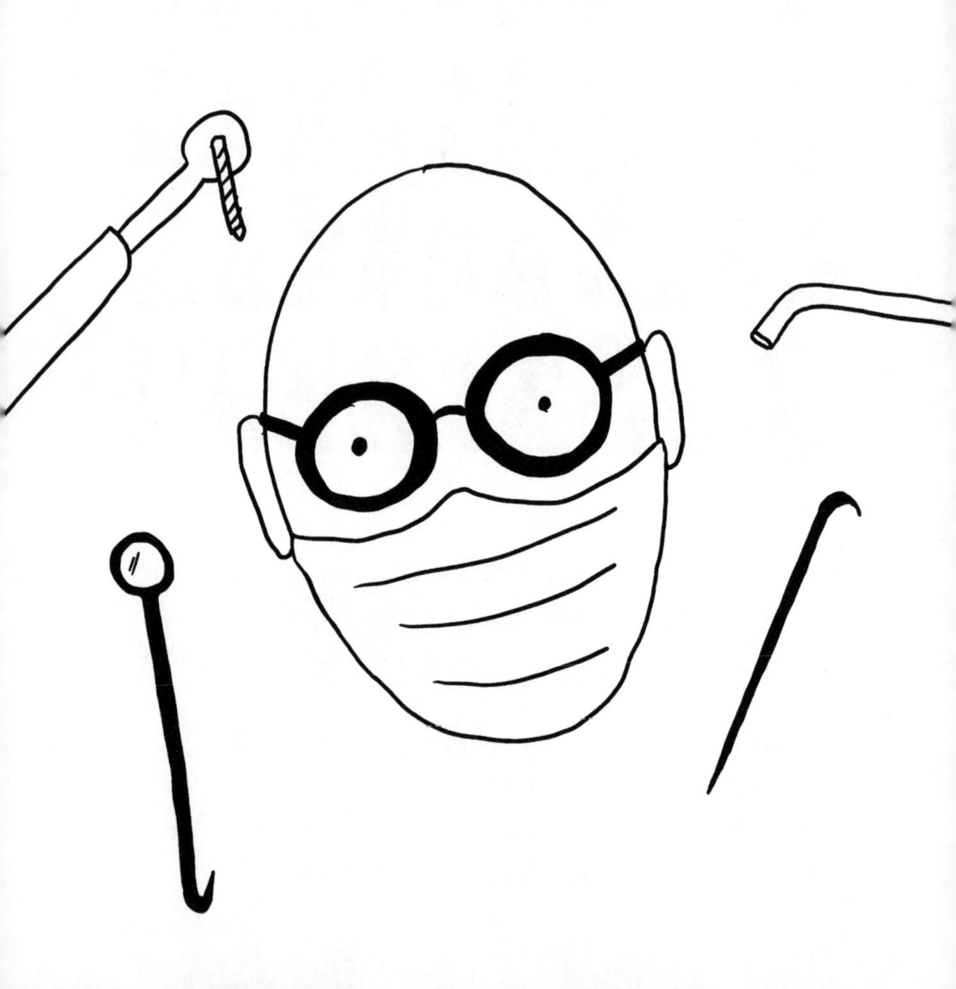

Dentists are terrible.

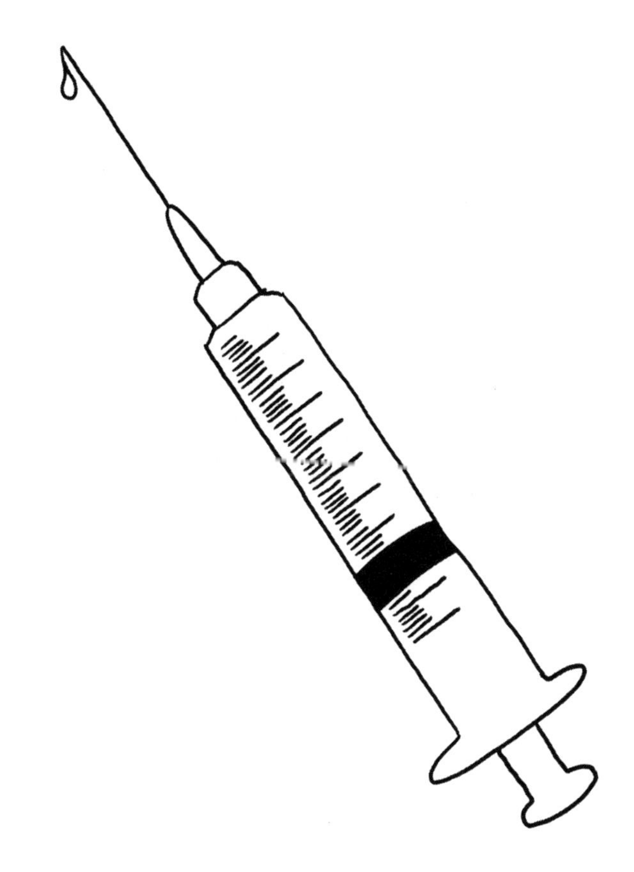

It's terrible when you are the only person who has to work late.

It's terrible that I'll never climb the corporate ladder.

It's terrible that I'm afraid of heights.

It's terrible when your job is a joke, but nobody is laughing.

This is a tough list to whittle down, but what are the top 3 worst things about your job that are either going to drive you to quit or just make you keep driving one day and never return?

1. ______________________________

2. ______________________________

3. ______________________________

It's terrible when someone interrupts you with a quick question while eating lunch.

It's terrible there is no such thing as a quick work question.

It's terrible when the work microwave is all splattered with someone else's food.
It's terrible when they clean out the work fridge and throw away your lunch.
It's terrible that we all can't work from home.
It's terrible that I can't even get all my work at home done.
It's terrible when nighttime is the only time you have to actually get work done.

It's terrible that we need to work.
It's terrible that it's called work.
It's terrible when you have to drag yourself to work.
It's terrible when you bring your work home with you.
It's terrible when you calculate how many more years there are until you can retire.
It's terrible if you won't have enough saved when you plan to retire.
It's terrible that we have to work to survive.
It's terrible that my job will likely kill me.

Its terrible that, thanks too autocorrect, we doesn't even need to learned how to spell.

It's terrible that my ninth-grade English teacher told me that I'd never become an author.

It's terrible (and slightly funny) that people will rate this book as 1 star, because they are trying to be funny by saying how terrible it is.

It's terrible if you don't have a sense of humor.

It's terrible that this book likely won't win any major awards.

It's terrible when you still have hope.

★☆☆☆☆

This book is so terrible that I lit it on fire and spread the ashes at the dump.

It's terrible when they underestimate what you can do.
It's terrible when YOU underestimate what you can do.
It's terrible when you don't get enough credit for what you do do.
It's terrible that I just made you say "doo-doo."
It's terrible how much crap we take.
It's terrible how much crap we are able to take.
It's terrible that we don't give it right back.
It's terrible when we don't give a crap anymore.

It's terrible when the forecast doesn't look good.
It's terrible when it's the same sh*t, different day.
It's terrible when it's new sh*t, same day.

Fill in the blank:

Yesterday: Everything was terrible.

Today: Everything is terrible.

Tomorrow: Everything will be

____.

It's terrible when people try to test you.

It's terrible when they censor photos.

It's terrible when they bleep curse words.

It's terrible when you curse in front of your parents for the first time.

It's terrible that I've learned all my swear words from my parents.

It's terrible when you hear someone use a bad word…who never curses.

We all have them, our favorite little impactful 4-letter words. It's likely pretty terrible, but what is your favorite 4-letter doozy of a word? Write each letter in one of the 4 boxes:

It's terrible when there is one too many.

It’s terrible when you can’t possibly do any more.
It’s terrible when you do manage to do more, then that becomes the new norm.
It’s terrible when you’ve reached your boiling point.
It’s terrible when you’ve exceeded your breaking point.
It’s terrible when there is no bright side to look to.
It’s terrible when the sun doesn’t come out tomorrow.
It’s terrible when you want people to choke on their #$@&ing inspirational quotes.

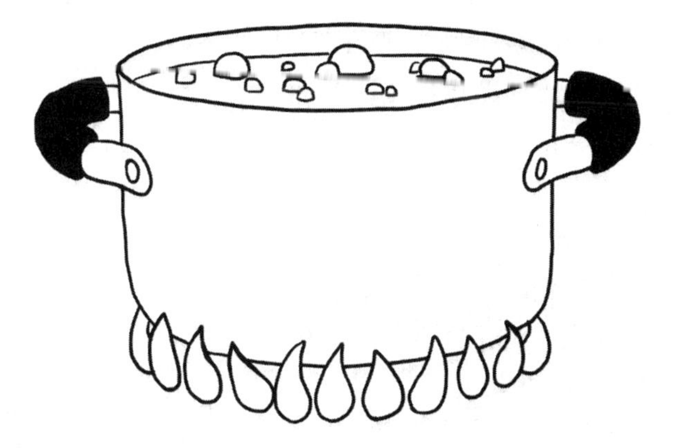

It's terrible that we are attracted to bad boys or naughty girls.

It's terrible when we don't learn the first time around.

It's terrible when we convince ourselves that something is a good idea.

It’s terrible when you have to lie.
It’s terrible when they believe everything you tell them.
It’s terrible when you forget which lie you used.
It’s terrible when you want nothing more than to lie down.
It’s terrible when you get stuck in a web of your own lies.
It’s terrible when you walk into a spiderweb.
It would be terrible if spiders were bigger.

Fears

It's terrible that I grew up being afraid of quicksand.
It's terrible that I'm still afraid of the dark.
It's terrible that I'll always be afraid of sharks.
It's terrible when you enjoy scary movies, but then can't sleep for days.

There are a lot of scary things out there, and we likely worry more about them than we need to. Out of the following terrible (and terrifying) things that scare most people, number in ascending order (1–13) what freaks you out the most.

Swimming in nature
Monsters
Creepy clowns
Darkness
Thunderstorms
Death
Being alone
Wild animals
Ghosts/ poltergeists
Fire
Slithery Things
Alien abductions
Demons
It's terrible that I believe pulling the covers up over my eyes will save me.

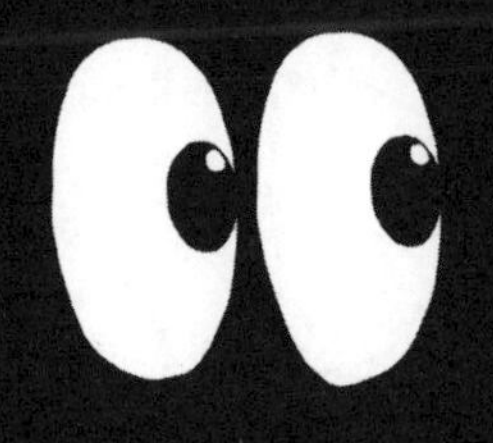

It's terrible that some days
you just want to go home,
turn off the lights
and sit quietly,
alone in the dark.

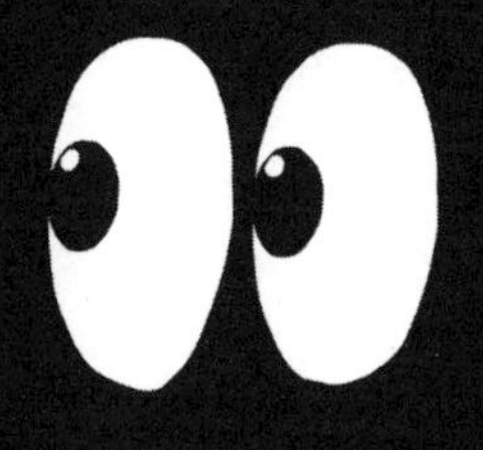

It's terrible when you
aren't alone.

It’d be terrible when you dig your own hole.

It’s terrible when the hole you’re in is so deep you can’t get out.

It’s terrible when you’ve hit rock bottom.

It’s terrible when no matter how hard you try, you keep falling further behind.

It’s terrible when there is no end.

It's terrible when you don't get a break.
It's terrible when your water breaks.
It's terrible when your balloon pops.
It's terrible when someone bursts your bubble.
It's terrible that there is actually a show on TV where
you can watch a doctor pop pimples.
It's terrible how addicting reality TV can be.
It's terrible how much our standards have declined.

Reality TV

It's terrible how addicting Hallmark and Lifetime movies are to watch.
It's terrible that every Hallmark and Lifetime movie has the same exact plot in the same perfect little town just outside of the big city.
It's terrible that every Hallmark and Lifetime movie shares the same three semi-famous movie stars.
It's terrible when you see the favorite movie stars of your lifetime looking really old.
It's terrible that fiction is more fun than reality.

What's worse than the Lifetime stories are the titles of the movies themselves and the cast that they get. If you were to name your terrible life story, what would be the title of your all-too-real Lifetime movie...and who would play the people in your life?

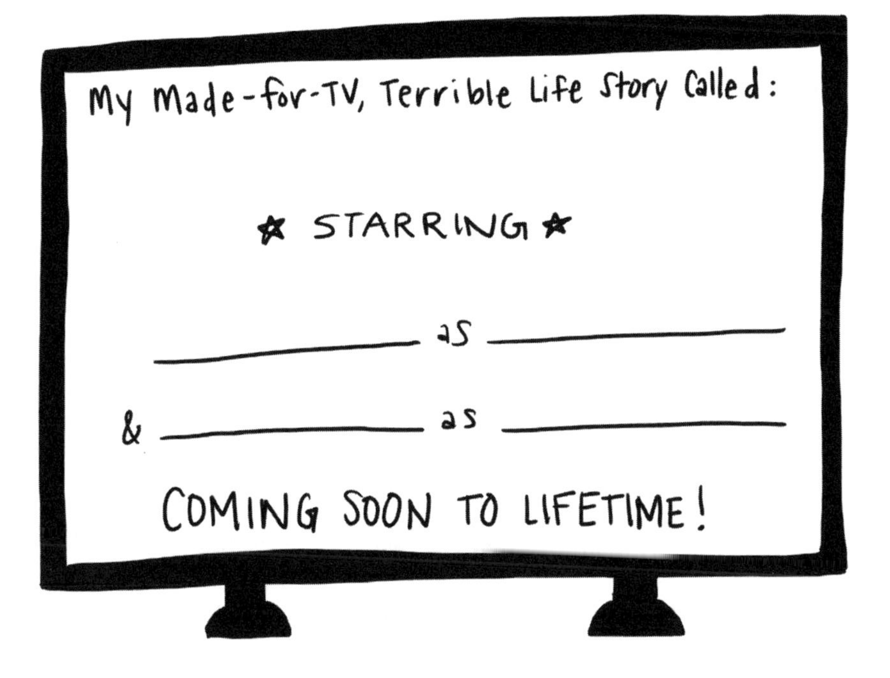

It’s terrible that my life story would go straight to video.

It’s terrible that I spend more time watching Lifetime than living life.

Kick the Bucket

It's terrible that I'll never climb Mt. Everest.
It's terrible that I'll never surf the Pipeline in Hawaii.
It's terrible if you never try.
It's terrible if you die trying.

We all have bucket list items that we would like to do someday...if we had the time, the money...and the ability to face our fears. But it's terrible that, in our short existence, for whatever reason, we'll miss out on some amazing life experiences that are available to us all.

What are some things on your list that you will likely never do before you kick the bucket?

It's terrible that things will likely always be terrible…
until the end.

It's terrible when there is no upside.

It's terrible when you can't
turn that frown upside down.

It's terrible when you don't know
which end is up.

It's terrible when you can only see
something from one point of view.

It's terrible when not much more
can go wrong.

It's terrible when it's
"famous last words."

It’s terrible when you expect something to be terrible.
It’s terrible when something IS usually terrible.
It’s terrible when something is UNUSUALLY terrible.
It’s terrible when something SHOULD BE terrible…then
it’s not.
It’s terrible when EVERYTHING is terrible.

The Final Countdown

It'd be terrible if an asteroid brought us unexpected Armageddon.

It'd be terrible if the Avengers were unable to save us from an otherworldly attack.

It'd be terrible if we are all just one big experiment, and they gave up on us.

It's always terrible when movies end leaving the ending to your interpretation.

One way or another, our entire existence as we know it will come to an end someday. We're unsure how and when, and though terrible for those who will be around to witness it, if you think about it, it will also finally put an end to everything that has been terrible up to that point.

So, while looking back in those final moments and throughout this book, as only we would do together, write down your TOP 5 TERRIBLE THINGS OF THEM ALL that you won't miss when the world is gone.

MY TOP 05 MOST TERRIBLE THINGS ARE:

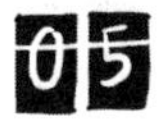

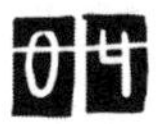

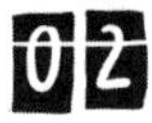

And THE WORST thing of them all is:

01

It's terrible when it ends faster than you expected.

The End.

It's terrible that we work so hard and can't take anything with us when we go.
It's terrible that we have all this time and do so little with it.
It's terrible that the end is nearer every day.
It's terrible when good things come to an end.
It's terrible when terrible things don't come to an end.

When the end finally comes for you, which is terrible in itself, if you could leave behind a few final parting words inscribed on your tombstone...how would it read?

It's terrible that this book is over, and everything is still terrible...if not worse.

It's terrible when you've reached the end.

It's terrible when you
want more.

It's terrible
when it doesn't have
a happy ending.

It's FAR from over for YOU...

When we say everything is terrible, it's nearly impossible to fit EVERYTHING in just four hundred pages. So it would be terrible if we didn't give you a place to share your terrible things and completed activities with us…and the world.

As your final activity...

1. **Use the following blank page to create your own Terrible Things List.**
2. **Add your personal artistic pizazz or maybe a creative border.**
3. **Snap a pic of it, or your favorite pages of this book, and anything else terrible.**
4. **Share it as #EverythingIsTerrible with us at:**
   Facebook: **Everything Is Terrible Book**
   Instagram: **@EverythingIsTerribleBook**

Also check out what other terribly funtastic things there are to loathe at TheHatePage.com!

#EverythingIsTerrible

Acknowledgments?

Unfortunately, a book like this writes itself when you have a world that feeds you nonstop juicy inspiration. With that in mind, I'm confused if I should give acknowledgment or not to all those who have inspired endless strings of terribleness. Regardless, there are some I should thank, or I may end up in their book complaining about me.

First, thanks to Brendan O'Neill of Adams Media for thinking of me, the guy who "hates everyone and everything," to write Rebecca Thomas's wonderfully terrible book idea. I ***think*** I'm flattered that I fit this role better than most.

Thanks also to my very talented partners in crime, Katie and Lis, for their skillful editing, artistry, and support for now more than 1,200 pages of terrible and hate-filled fun.

I would also like to acknowledge my wonderful family, friends, and especially my wife, Jen, for supporting and commiserating along with me every miserable day.

And lastly, special thanks to my beloved fridge, which has supported my stress eating while I dove deep into a world of everything terrible, and finally, to my dog Kona, for raising an eyebrow every time I chuckled at the insanity of it all.

A Little about the Author

With a resume of published books that include *Everything Is Terrible.*, *I Hate Everything.*, and *I Hate Everyone.*, Matthew DiBenedetti's "Mr. Positive, feel-good" reputation is starting to get tarnished. Normally in conversation or with clients, when people excitedly ask, "Oh, you're published; what's the name of your books?" it would be a pleasant conversation, but as the authority of hate and everything terrible, Matt is getting used to the "uncertain-what-to-say" looks people give him when they find out what he's written.

It's no matter what anyone thinks; Matt knows he's not alone. He enjoys his fans who appreciate his dark little sense of humor, and that's all that matters. Everything else …is terrible.